LAUBACH WAY TO English 3

A time-tested method that has taught millions of adults to read

TEACHER'S GUIDE
to Using Laubach Way to Reading with ESL Students

JEANETTE D. MACERO

New Readers Press
ProLiteracy's publishing division

Laubach Way to English 3
Teacher's Guide to Using *Laubach Way to Reading* with ESL Students
ISBN 978-1-56420-941-2

Copyright © 2011, 1991, 1985 New Readers Press
New Readers Press
ProLiteracy's Publishing Division
104 Marcellus Street, Syracuse, New York 13204
www.newreaderspress.com

All rights reserved. No part of this book may be reproduced or transmitted in any form or by any means, electronic or mechanical, including photocopying, recording, or by any information storage and retrieval system, without permission in writing from the publisher.

Printed in the United States of America
9 8 7 6 5 4 3

Proceeds from the sale of New Readers Press materials support professional development, training, and technical assistance programs of ProLiteracy that benefit local literacy programs in the U.S. and around the globe.

Developmental Editor: Terrie Lipke
Creative Director: Andrea Woodbury
Production Specialist: Maryellen Casey
Art and Design Supervisor: James P. Wallace
Cover Design: Carolyn Wallace

Table of Contents

© New Readers Press. All rights reserved.

Series Overview

Laubach Way to English is a series of teacher's guides designed for teaching English as a second language (ESL). Each teacher's guide is correlated to a *Laubach Way to Reading* student skill book. The skill book is the student's text-workbook in reading and writing. The materials provide a comprehensive beginning English program in listening, speaking, reading, and writing skills.

Laubach Way to Reading

The *Laubach Way to Reading* series is a basic reading and writing series, developed primarily for adults with little or no reading ability. The series, which begins at the zero level of literacy, consists of four skill books. Each book is followed by a correlated reader that gives additional practice in sustained reading.

Laubach Way to Reading has four levels:

- Book 1: Sounds and Names of Letters
- Book 2: Short Vowel Sounds
- Book 3: Long Vowel Sounds
- Book 4: Other Vowel Sounds and Consonant Spellings

Components Needed for Level 3

The student's reading materials for this level are *Laubach Way to Reading 3* and the correlated reader *Changes*. Two teacher's guides are required:

- To teach listening and speaking skills at level 3, use this *Laubach Way to English Teacher's Guide 3*. Practice in listening and speaking conversation skills includes dialogs, vocabulary, grammatical structures, and listening exercises. These skills are sequenced systematically so that the student has thorough aural-oral practice with vocabulary and grammatical structures before meeting them in the reading. Additional vocabulary and structures, not found in the reading, are provided for their usefulness in everyday life. *Laubach Way to Reading Workbook 3* is designed to give students additional practice in listening to, speaking, reading, and writing English. *Laubach Way to English Illustrations 3*, a teacher's picture book available on our website, may be used in conjunction with this guide to show the student the meaning of new vocabulary.
- To teach reading and writing skills, use *Laubach Way to Reading Teacher's Edition 3*. It is written for *all* students using the skill books—both native speakers and ESL students—so you may need to adapt the suggested teacher's instructions to the student somewhat for your ESL student's comprehension.

Cursive writing is also taught at this level, beginning in Lesson 22. For this, you will need the student workbook *The Laubach Way to Cursive Writing* and the accompanying teacher's guide. For students who already know cursive writing, *LWR Teacher's Edition 3* provides alternative writing lessons.

Two evaluations of student progress complete level 3. The "Oral Evaluation for Book 3," which checks the student's progress in conversation skills, is found at the end of this guide. To evaluate the student's progress in reading and writing, use *Checkups 3*, available on our website. Directions for administering and scoring these checkups are at the end of *LWR Teacher's Edition 3*.

Meeting the Needs of ESL Students

Laubach Way to Reading was originally written for adult native speakers of English with little or no reading skills. The *Laubach Way to English* teacher's guides were developed to adapt the books for ESL instruction. The ESL guides for levels 1 and 2, besides providing instruction in conversation skills, also adapted the instructions for teaching reading and writing to the easy wording that beginning ESL students could understand. Level 3 students, in contrast, should be able to understand the verbal instructions suggested in the regular *LWR Teacher's Edition 3* with only a little adaptation.

Although the materials were designed specifically for teaching adults who are illiterate in their native language as well as in English, they can be used successfully with many other ESL students. In particular, literate students whose native languages have writing systems other than the Roman alphabet should find the practice in basic reading and writing skills beneficial.

Each One Teach One, and Classrooms Too

Among other things, the Laubach method has traditionally meant "Each One Teach One," a volunteer tutor and a student, teaching and learning in an atmosphere of caring and compassion.

Accordingly, the methods described in the *Laubach Way to English* apply to a one-to-one teaching situation, but suggestions are offered for adapting the methods for small-group or classroom use. Thus, the series is useful for ESL-ABE classes in public schools as well as for tutoring programs.

For volunteer tutors and beginning teachers

The detailed step-by-step instructions in both the *Laubach Way to English* and *Laubach Way to Reading* teacher's guides make it possible for both volunteer tutors and beginning ESL teachers to use the material with ease and confidence.

© New Readers Press. All rights reserved.

Lesson Notes Overview

General Procedures

This guide is meant to be used after the student has successfully completed the material in *Laubach Way to English 2.*

Placing the new student

A new student who seems to have some knowledge of English should not be placed directly in book 3 without careful evaluation. Many times, a student has acquired some superficial fluency in carrying on simple conversations. This can be misleading, since often such a student does not have a mastery of the basic structural patterns of English.

It is best to administer both the Oral Evaluation (Parts I and II) and the Reading and Writing Evaluation for book 2 to determine where in the series the student should begin. The teacher should evaluate the student's performance as directed.

Even if the student is ready to begin book 3, it would be wise to review any test items that caused him difficulty since each new lesson builds on all that has been taught in previous lessons.

Format of the lessons

The lessons in this guide are divided into two parts: Conversation Skills and Reading and Writing.

The Conversation Skills section begins with a dialog, which the student will find useful in both the learning situation and his daily life. This is followed by the vocabulary items to be taught and the structural patterns in which the words are to be used. Next, there is a pronunciation practice to give the student some flexibility in making the sounds of English. This section ends with an oral evaluation, or review, of the new material.

The Reading and Writing section directs you to the student book lesson and the *LWR* Teacher's Edition notes for the lesson.

Lesson Notes Style

Slash Marks. Slash marks around a letter or letters indicate the sound for which they stand. Thus, you say /g/ like the beginning consonant sound in *girl*, and /j/ like the beginning consonant sound in *jumping*.

Italics. Letters in italics are read by their letter names, as: *a, b, c*.

Pronouns referring to teacher and student. Although the authors recognize that there are teachers and students of both sexes, they have chosen, for the sake of brevity, to use the pronoun *she* to refer to the teacher and *he* to refer to the student.

© New Readers Press. All rights reserved.

Lesson Notes for Book 3

Lesson 1

OBJECTIVES

When a student completes this lesson, he should be able to:

1. Say and respond to a new dialog.
2. Say the chart words plus some words concerning music.
3. Recognize some music.
4. Say the names of animals and meats derived from the animals.
5. Say some story words, especially food items.
6. Use some irregular verbs in past tense statements.
7. Listen to a story and repeat it in his own words.

VISUAL AIDS

1. *LWE Illustrations 3*, pp. 2–4.
2. A tape or recording of a song.

I. Conversation Skills

DIALOG

David:	What are you going to order?
Jason:	I'm not very hungry. I'll have a snack.
David:	I won't eat much either. I'm on a diet.
Jason:	Sounds good. Here comes the waitress.
Waitress:	May I take your order?
David:	I'll have a salad and a diet soda.
Jason:	I'll have a ham sandwich and a cup of coffee.
Waitress:	Anything else?
Jason:	Not for now. Thanks.

Instructions to the teacher

Note: The procedure for teaching the dialog is the same as in *Laubach Way to English Teacher's Guides 1* and *2*.

1. Model the entire dialog two or three times while the student listens.
   a. Do not say the words *David, Jason*, or *Waitress*.
   b. Explain vocabulary the student may not know; for example, *on a diet* means to eat less, to get thinner.
   c. Indicate appropriate pictures of a salad, a sandwich, and a soda as they occur in the dialog.
   d. To change roles, shift your weight from one foot to the other, and turn your body slightly.

2. Model each line of the dialog, having the student repeat it after you.

   Class: In a class situation, first have the class repeat in unison. Then divide the class into groups, and have each group repeat. Have members of the class begin each line of the dialog exactly at the same time, or there will be utter confusion.

© New Readers Press. All rights reserved.

3. Take one role of the dialog, and have the student take the others.

4. Reverse roles.

Class: For steps 3–4, have the members of the class say the dialog in unison, then in pairs. In a large class, divide the class in half, with each half taking first one, then the other role in the dialog. Then divide the class into quarters, ending with one-to-one practice. (In a dialog like this one with three speakers, divide the class into three groups, then six, and end with one-to-one practice.)

Keep the pace brisk. Praise your students often.

VOCABULARY: Music

I listen to music on the radio.
The singer is singing a song.
The song is ____________________.

---

1. Teacher models the sentences and plays a song. Student listens.

   Note: Teacher explains the vocabulary by indicating the singer and the name of the song being played.

2. Teacher models each sentence. Student repeats after each sentence.

   Note: You may sing the words of the song or play a tape or recording of it. Use a well-known popular song. Avoid songs with difficult vocabulary, however.

3. Teacher and student sing the song together.

VOCABULARY: Meat and Animals

This is a lamb.
This is a cow.
This is a pig.
This is a chicken.
We eat the meat from these animals.
We eat beef. Beef and hamburger come from cows.
We eat pork and ham. Pork and ham come from pigs.
We eat lamb. It comes from lambs.
We eat chicken. It comes from chickens.

---

1. Teacher models all the sentences, using *LWE Illustrations 3*, pp. 2–3.

2. Teacher models the sentences. Student repeats each sentence.

DRILL: Identification Drill

Teacher points to the illustrations and asks, "What's this?" Also, teacher asks, "Where do beef and hamburger come from?" and similar questions.

© New Readers Press. All rights reserved.

VOCABULARY: Food Items

Mrs. Falco goes to the supermarket to buy food for three meals: breakfast, lunch, and dinner.

She buys eggs, milk, and butter for breakfast.
She buys bread, ham, and cheese to make sandwiches for lunch.
She buys hamburger, beans, coffee, and tea for dinner.
She buys lettuce and tomatoes for a salad.

The food costs $30.00. The price of the food is $30.00.
Mrs. Falco pays her bill and goes home.

---

1. Teacher models each sentence using actual objects or the pictures on pp. 4–5 of *LWE Illustrations 3*. Student listens.
2. Teacher models each sentence, having the student repeat.

DRILL: Identification Drill

Teacher has student identify food items by asking the student "What's this?" and using the objects or pictures on pp. 4–5 of *LWE Illustrations 3*.

Note: Prompt the student only when necessary. Review all previous words after each new word.

DRILL: Question and Answer Drill

Teacher asks questions to elicit vocabulary items. The student does not have to name every item that would be a correct answer.

Model the first two items, having the student repeat only the answer.

Teacher	**Student**
Why does Mrs. Falco go to the supermarket? She goes to buy food for breakfast, lunch, and dinner.	She goes to buy food for breakfast, lunch, and dinner.
What does Mrs. Falco buy for lunch? She buys bread, ham, and cheese.	She buys bread, ham, and cheese.
What kind of sandwiches will Mrs. Falco make? What does Mrs. Falco buy for dinner? What does Mrs. Falco buy to make a salad? What does Mrs. Falco buy to drink?	
Why does Mrs. Falco buy lettuce and tomatoes? How much does the food cost? How much was Mrs. Falco's bill? What is the price of the food?	

© New Readers Press. All rights reserved.

STRUCTURE FOCUS: Past Tense of Irregular Verbs

Present	Past
Carla Lopez sends a letter to her mother every week.	Carla Lopez sent a letter to her mother last week.
I spend $1.00 to ride the bus every week.	I spent $1.00 to ride the bus last week.
Jason lends his book to David every week.	Jason lent his book to David last week.
Carla cuts the grass every week.	Carla cut the grass two weeks ago.
He puts money in the bank every week.	He put $10.00 in the bank last week.
He shuts the door when he comes in.	He shut the door when he came in.

1. Teacher models each pair of sentences, saying first the present tense and then the past tense. Act out verbs the student does not know. Student listens.
2. Teacher models each sentence. Student repeats after each sentence.

Note: Be sure the student notices that there is only an *-s* ending difference between the third person present and past tense forms of *cost*, *cut*, *shut*, and *put*.

DRILL: Transformation Drill

Teacher gives a present tense statement.
Student changes it into a past tense statement.

Teacher	Student
I send a letter to my mother every week. I sent a letter to my mother last week.	I sent a letter to my mother last week.
Ed cuts the grass every week. Ed cut the grass last week.	Ed cut the grass last week.

I lend my car to Jason.
The book costs $8.95 now.
Ed cuts the grass every week.
She puts her glasses in her purse.
Jason sends a letter to Ed every week.
Carla lends her jacket to Ann.
Ed shuts the door every day.

© New Readers Press. All rights reserved.

DRILL: Answering Questions

Teacher asks student questions which he answers in the past tense.

Teacher	Student
What did David lend Tom? He lent him a book.	He lent him a book.
What did you send your mother? I sent her some money.	I sent her some money.
Where did you put your coat?	
What did you lend Carla?	
How much did the book cost?	
Who cut the bread?	
How much did Jason spend for food?	
When did you lend Carla your book?	
When did Ed shut the door?	

© New Readers Press. All rights reserved.

STRUCTURE FOCUS: *before* and *after*

Before work, I had breakfast.
Before watching TV, I had dinner.
Before class, I read my book.

After work, I had dinner.
After watching TV, I went to bed.
After class, I went home.

1. Teacher models each sentence, asking the student to listen to *before* or *after*. Student listens.
2. Teacher models each sentence. Student repeats after each sentence.

DRILL: Question and Answer Drill

Teacher asks these questions: "What did you do *before* class?" and "What did you do *after* class?" Student replies may vary.

Teacher	Student
What did you do before class?	
I read my book before class.	I read my book before class,
What did you do after eating a snack?	
I went to bed after eating a snack.	I went to bed after eating a snack.

What did you do before work?
What did you do before class?
What did you do before dinner?
What did you do before watching TV?
What did you do before going to bed?

What did you do after work?
What did you do after class?
What did you do after dinner?
What did you do after watching TV?
What did you do after eating a snack?

LISTENING COMPREHENSION

Jason and Carla went to Fran's Snack Shop. They were hungry. Jason ordered a ham sandwich. They both drank milk. They said the food was good.

1. Teacher reads the story twice at a normal pace.
   Student listens. Student asks about words he does not know.
2. Student tells the story in his own words. If the student cannot tell the story, teacher may begin the sentence and have the student complete it.

© New Readers Press. All rights reserved.

ORAL EVALUATION

It is recommended that the teacher have a notebook for recording the student's progress. It is especially necessary to make notes about items that a student is having difficulty with so that you can review the items at the beginning of the next session.

When possible, the number of vocabulary items the student should be able to name is indicated. For most reviews of structure focus drills, the student should be able to respond fairly quickly. If he needs prompting to any great extent, make a note, and review the structure at the next session.

Follow these procedures for the oral evaluation at the end of each lesson.

1. Have the student say the words about music and say the words of the song (if you taught a song).
2. Using *LWE Illustrations 3*, pp. 2–3, have the student identify the names of the animals and the meats derived from them by doing the Identification Drill. Student should be able to name 8 items.
3. Using *LWE Illustrations 3*, pp. 4–5, do the Question and Answer Drill about food items. Student should be able to name 7 items.
4. Have the student review the present and past tense of irregular verbs by doing the Transformation Drill. Student should know the past tense of each verb.

II. Reading and Writing

BOOK 3: Lesson 1

Complete Lesson 1 in book 3, following the instructions given in *Laubach Way to Reading Teacher's Edition 3*. Adapt the wording of the suggested teacher's instructions to the student as needed for your ESL student's comprehension.

ADDITIONAL WRITTEN PRACTICE

After completing Lesson 1 in book 3, have the student do the practices for Lesson 1 in workbook 3.

Note: Workbook 3 is designed to give ESL students in particular additional practice in the patterns presented in book 3. The vocabulary is controlled to the reading vocabulary the student has learned at each lesson level in book 3, although some new words are introduced. Before assigning any material in workbook 3, read the introductory section called "To the Teacher" for an explanation of how to use the exercises.

© New Readers Press. All rights reserved.

Lesson 2

OBJECTIVES

When a student completes this lesson, he should be able to:

1. Say and respond to a new dialog.
2. Say some words about work.
3. Say some names of vegetables.
4. Say some liquid measures and food in quantities.
5. Use the structure *it* + *be*, as in *It's sunny*.
6. Use the structure *it* for identification, as in *Who is it? It's Ed.*
7. Use the present perfect tense with *ever* and *never*.
8. Listen to a story and repeat it in his own words.

VISUAL AIDS

1. *LWE Illustrations 3*, pp. 4–8.
2. Bring some rice, plus color pictures of these vegetables or the actual vegetables:

tomatoes	carrots	onions	beans
lettuce	potatoes	peas	

3. Measuring cup that shows 1/4 and 1/2 cup markings.

I. Conversation Skills

DIALOG

Carla:	I don't know what to cook for dinner tonight.
Mrs. King:	How about chicken with instant rice and a salad?
Carla:	What's instant rice?
Mrs. King:	It's rice that cooks very fast. It's easy to cook.
Carla:	It sounds good. Would you like to have dinner with us?
Mrs. King:	No, thanks. Not tonight. I have to work.

1. Model the entire dialog two or three times. Student listens.
2. Model each line. Student repeats after each line.
3. Teacher takes one role of the dialog. Student takes the other.
4. Reverse roles.
5. Vary the dialog by practicing with other menus the student may suggest.

© New Readers Press. All rights reserved.

VOCABULARY: Words about Work

Ray has a full-time job in a paper factory.
He works 40 hours a week.

Kay has two part-time jobs.

She is a babysitter.
She babysits for 15 hours every week.

She is a clerk in a department store.
She works there 15 hours every week.

1. While student listens, teacher models each sentence, using *LWE Illustrations 3*, p. 8, to show the new words *babysitter* and *clerk*. Explain that a full-time job is 35–40 hours of work per week, and a part-time job is less than that.
2. Teacher models the sentences. Student repeats after each sentence.

VOCABULARY: Vegetables

Many people eat vegetables.
They eat tomatoes.
They eat lettuce.
They eat carrots.
They eat potatoes.
They eat peas.
They eat onions.
They eat rice.
They eat beans.

Note: You may wish to add other vegetables, depending on what foods are part of your student's diet, e.g., eggplant, corn, cabbage, cucumber, celery, or green pepper.

1. Teacher models each sentence, using rice and other actual vegetables, color photos, or *LWE Illustrations 3*, pp. 4–7, to show the new words.
2. Teacher models the sentences. Student repeats after each sentence.

DRILL: Identification Drill

Teacher points to the illustrations of vegetables and asks, "What's this?" or "What do people eat?"

© New Readers Press. All rights reserved.

VOCABULARY: Liquid Measures

This is a cup.
This is a half cup.
This is a quarter cup.

---

1. Teacher models each sentence, using a measuring cup or *LWE Illustrations 3*, p. 7, to show the new words.
2. Teacher models the sentences. Student repeats after each sentence.

VOCABULARY: Food in Quantities

Mrs. Falco buys a stick of butter.
She puts a pat of butter on her bread.
She buys a head of lettuce.
She buys a can of peas.
She buys a pound of hamburger.
She buys a quart of milk.

---

1. While student listens, teacher models each sentence, using actual objects or *LWE Illustrations 3*, pp. 4–7, to show the new words.
2. Teacher models the sentences. Student repeats after each sentence.

© New Readers Press. All rights reserved.

STRUCTURE FOCUS: *It + be*

It's half past six.
It's a nice day today. It's sunny.
It was rainy yesterday.
It's June.
It's fun to play cards.

1. Teacher models each sentence, asking the student to listen to *It's* and *It was.*
2. Teacher models the sentence. Student repeats after each sentence.

DRILL: Completion Drill

1. Teacher gives part of a sentence.
   Student completes the sentences by using *It's* and *It was.*
2. Teacher models the first two items. Student listens.

Note: Conduct each drill in this book in this manner. These instructions will not be repeated for each drill after this.

Teacher	Student
half past six It's half past six.	It's half past six.
sunny yesterday It was sunny yesterday.	It was sunny yesterday.

rainy today
June
Monday
7 o'clock
easy to play cards
hard to make ice cream
fun to go fishing yesterday
easy to make a cake
a nice day today

© New Readers Press. All rights reserved.

STRUCTURE FOCUS: *It* for Identification

Who is it at the door?	It's Carla and David.
Who was it on the telephone?	It was Anne.

1. Teacher models each question with its answer. Student listens.
2. Teacher models each question and answer. Student repeats after each item.

DRILL: Completion Drill

Teacher gives part of a sentence.
Student completes the sentence by using *It's* or *It was*.

Teacher	**Student**
Ed It's Ed.	It's Ed.
Carla and David It's Carla and David.	It's Carla and David.

Anne on the telephone yesterday
a woman at the door
a man on the telephone last night
your mother
your sister and brother
me
Rosa on the telephone
Jason at the door last night

© New Readers Press. All rights reserved.

STRUCTURE FOCUS: Present Perfect Tense with *ever* and *never*

Have you ever painted a house?
No, I have never painted a house.

Have you ever fixed stairs?
No, I have never fixed stairs.

Have you ever spent $200 for food?
No, I have never spent $200 for food.

Have you ever sent a letter to the president?
No, I have never sent a letter to the president.

Have you ever lent anyone your car?
No, I have never lent anyone my car.

---

1. Teacher models the sentences in pairs, the question with *ever* and the answer with *never*.
2. Teacher models each question and its answer. Student repeats after each item.

DRILL: Answering Questions

Teacher asks student questions with *ever* which he answers in the negative with *never*.

Teacher	Student
Have you ever painted your house? No, I have never painted my house.	No, I have never painted my house.
Have you ever fixed stairs? No, I have never fixed stairs.	No, I have never fixed stairs.

Have you ever sent Carla a letter?
Have you ever lent Ed any money?
Have you ever spent a lot of money in one day?
Have you ever lent anyone your car?
Have you ever lived in New York?
Have you ever lived in a big apartment?
Have you ever washed a dog?
Have you ever painted stairs?

© New Readers Press. All rights reserved.

DRILL: Making Questions

Teacher gives words which student must use in the question form
Have you ever...?

Teacher	**Student**
painted a house Have you ever painted a house?	Have you ever painted a house?
fixed stairs Have you ever fixed stairs?	Have you ever fixed stairs?
spent a lot of money sent Carla a letter lent Ed some money fixed a chair lived in New York washed a dog	

Note: Drill can be varied by having student make questions about Jason: "Has Jason ever painted a house?" Continue with the remaining items.

LISTENING COMPREHENSION

Carla Lopez lives in an apartment in a big building. She works at a music shop. She has worked there for six years.

Carla has a baby. Her baby's name is Rosa. Rosa is two. Mrs. King is Rosa's babysitter. She babysits Rosa while Carla is at work.

1. Teacher reads the story twice at a normal pace. Student listens. Student asks about words he does not know.
2. Student tells the story in his own words. If the student cannot tell the story, teacher may begin the sentence and have the student complete it.

Note: If the student cannot remember the story, read it once or twice again.

© New Readers Press. All rights reserved.

ORAL EVALUATION

1. Using *LWE Illustrations 3*, p. 8, have your student identify the words about work. He should be able to identify all of them.
2. Using *LWE Illustrations 3*, pp. 4–6, have your student identify the vegetables. He should be able to name 7 of them fairly quickly.
3. Using *LWE Illustrations 3*, p. 7, have your student identify the liquid measures. He should be able to name all of them.
4. Using *LWE Illustrations 3*, pp. 4–7, have your student identify foods in quantity. He should be able to name 5 of them.
5. Review the present perfect tense with *ever* and *never*. Do the drill on Making Questions, and have the student answer.

II. Reading and Writing

BOOK 3: Lesson 2

Complete Lesson 2 in book 3, following the instructions given in *Laubach Way to Reading Teacher's Edition 3*. Adapt the wording of the suggested teacher's instructions to the student as needed for your ESL student's comprehension.

Note: In this lesson and following lessons, you may need especially to adapt the oral comprehension questions suggested for each story. You may need to change the wording or to explain the meaning of any new vocabulary items or of idioms that your ESL student does not understand.

At times, you may need to explain some facet of American culture. For example, one question about the story in Lesson 2 asks, "Do you think the babysitter is about the same age as Carla or much older?" The answer is that the babysitter is probably much older because Carla calls her *Mrs.* instead of using her first name. Your ESL student may need to be told that American acquaintances of about the same age usually call each other by their first names, even if they are not very close friends. We usually use titles like *Mr.* and *Mrs.* only for persons who are much older or are in a much higher position.

If any oral comprehension question requires more explanation than you think its content is worth, feel free to omit it.

ADDITIONAL WRITTEN PRACTICE

After completing Lesson 2 in book 3, have the student do the practices for Lesson 2 in workbook 3.

© New Readers Press. All rights reserved.

Lesson 3

OBJECTIVES

When a student completes this lesson, he should be able to:

1. Say and respond to a new dialog.
2. Say words about getting paid and writing checks.
3. Use the verbs *play* + noun and *go* + verb-*ing* to indicate games and sports.
4. Use the structure *have to.*
5. Use *It* + adjective + infinitive, as in *It is fun to go camping.*
6. Listen to a story and repeat it in his own words.

VISUAL AIDS

1. *LWE Illustrations 3*, pp. 9–13.
2. An example of a personal check. (An old cancelled check will do.)

I. Conversation Skills

DIALOG

A: Hello, I'm calling about the apartment you advertised in the paper.
How many bedrooms are there?
B: Two. There's a big living room and a modern kitchen.

A: How much is it a month?
B: It's $500 a month plus utilities.

A: I'd like to think it over. I'll call you back.

---

1. Model the entire dialog two or three times. Student listens.

 Note: Explain that *utilities* include gas, lights, and heat.
 The word *plus* means "and" or "in addition to."

2. Model each line. Student repeats after each line.
3. Teacher takes one role of the dialog. Student takes the other.
4. Reverse roles.

© New Readers Press. All rights reserved.

VOCABULARY: Getting Paid and Writing Checks

Kay and Ray Mason have jobs.
They get paid twice a month.
They get $500 every payday.

Kay writes a check for their telephone bill.
Kay writes a check for the rent.
Kay gives the rent check to the landlady.

1. Teacher models each sentence, using *LWE Illustrations 3*, p. 9.
   Student listens.
2. Teacher models the sentences. Student repeats after each sentence.

DRILL: Question and Answer Drill

Teacher asks questions to elicit vocabulary items.

Teacher	Student
Who has a job? Kay and Ray Mason.	Kay and Ray Mason.
How often do Kay and Ray get paid? They get paid twice a month.	They get paid twice a month.

How much do Kay and Ray get every payday?
How do they pay their telephone bill?
Who do they pay their rent to?
When do Kay and Ray get five hundred dollars?
How often do Kay and Ray get paid?

© New Readers Press. All rights reserved.

VOCABULARY: The Verbs *play* and *go* with Games and Sports

play	go
They play cards.	They go camping.
They play football.	They go fishing.
They play baseball.	They go swimming.
They play basketball.	They go skiing.
They play hockey.	They go skating.

1. Teacher models all the sentences with *play*, then those with *go*. Use *LWE Illustrations 3*, pp. 10–13. Student listens.
2. Teacher models each sentence. Student repeats after each sentence.

Note: Some activities are expressed with *play* + noun, others with *go* + verb-*ing*. Student may ask you about other sports he knows.

DRILL: Completing Sentences

Teacher names an activity. Student uses it in a sentence with *play* or *go*.

Teacher	Student
cards We play cards.	We play cards.
camping We go camping.	We go camping.

football
basketball
swimming
fishing
skiing
baseball
skating
hockey

© New Readers Press. All rights reserved.

STRUCTURE FOCUS: *have to* + Simple Form of the Verb

I	have to	eat	dinner after work.
You	have to	stop	for a red light.
He	has to	call	Carla before dinner.
We	have to	work	tomorrow.

1. Teacher models each sentence, asking the student to listen to *have to* and *has to.*
2. Teacher models each sentence. Student repeats after each sentence.

DRILL: Question and Answer Drill

Teacher asks a question which the student answers using *have to.*
Student replies may vary.

Teacher	**Student**
What do you have to do after breakfast? I have to go to work.	I have to go to work.
What do you have to do tomorrow? I have to buy some food.	I have to buy some food.

What do you have to do after dinner?
What do you have to do after work?
What do you have to do today?
What do you have to do tomorrow?
What do you have to do after class?
What do you have to do before dinner?

© New Readers Press. All rights reserved.

STRUCTURE FOCUS: *It* + Adjective + Infinitive

It	is	fun	to go	camping.
It	is	easy	to play	cards.
It	is	hard	to pay	our bills.
It	is	nice	to be	with friends.

1. Teacher models each sentence, asking student to listen to *to go, to play*, etc. Student listens.
2. Teacher models each sentence. Student repeats after each sentence.

DRILL: Making Questions

Teacher gives words that student must use in the question form *Is it...?*
Student completes the question.

Teacher	**Student**
fun to go camping Is it fun to go camping?	Is it fun to go camping?
easy to play cards Is it easy to play cards?	Is it easy to play cards?

fun to go fishing
hard to pay your bills
nice to be with friends
fun to go camping
easy to play baseball

© New Readers Press. All rights reserved.

LISTING COMPREHENSION

Kay and Ray Mason like to play cards with their friends. They sometimes play cards with Carla and David. They have fun together.

Sometimes Kay and Ray go camping. They go camping in the woods. They go fishing. They have fun together.

---

1. Teacher reads the story twice at a normal pace.
   Student listens. Student asks about words he does not know.

2. Student tells the story in his own words. If the student cannot tell the story, teacher may begin the sentence and have the student complete it.

Note: If the student cannot remember the story, read it once or twice again.

ORAL EVALUATION

1. Using *LWE Illustrations 3*, p. 9, have the student identify the words about getting paid and writing checks by doing the Question and Answer Drill. Student should be able to answer all the questions.

2. Using *LWE Illustrations 3*, pp. 10–13, name the activity and have the student use it in a sentence with *play* or *go*. Student should know 6 of them.

3. Review *have to* + simple form of the verb by doing the Question and Answer Drill.

4. Review *It* + adjective + infinitive by doing the Making Questions Drill.

II. Reading and Writing

BOOK 3: Lesson 3

Complete Lesson 3 in book 3, following the instructions given in *Laubach Way to Reading Teacher's Edition 3*. Adapt the wording of the suggested teacher's instructions to the student as needed for your ESL student's comprehension.

ADDITIONAL WRITTEN PRACTICE

After completing Lesson 3 in book 3, have the student do the practices for Lesson 3 in workbook 3.

© New Readers Press. All rights reserved.

Lesson 4

OBJECTIVES

When a student completes this lesson, he should be able to:

1. Say and respond to a new dialog.
2. Say some words about basic tools and equipment.
3. Say the parts of the face.
4. Use *shall* in questions.
5. Use *when* clauses.
6. Use verb + infinitive, as in *I'll plan to go.*
7. Use verb + noun/pronoun + infinitive, as in *I'll ask them to come.*
8. Listen to a story and repeat it in his own words.

VISUAL AIDS

1. *LWE Illustrations 3*, pp. 14–16.
2. Any of these objects that it is convenient to bring:

hammer	pliers	saw	pail
nails	ladder	piece of wood	paint
screwdriver		scissors	paintbrush
screws		paper	

I. Conversation Skills

DIALOG

A: I want to fix this chair. It's broken.
B: You'll need a hammer and some nails.

A: I'll buy the nails at the store.
Will you help me fix the chair?
B: Sure. I'll be glad to.

Use actual objects or *LWE Illustrations 3*, pp. 14–15.

1. Model the entire dialog two or three times. Student listens.
2. Model each line. Student repeats after each line.
3. Teacher takes one role of the dialog. Student takes the other.
4. Reverse roles.

Note: Follow the same procedure for all dialogs in the following lessons.

© New Readers Press. All rights reserved.

VOCABULARY: Basic Tools and Equipment

We need a hammer and some nails.
We need a screwdriver and some screws.
We need a saw to cut wood.
We need pliers.
We need scissors to cut paper.
We need a ladder to climb to high places.
We need a pail to put water in.
We need some paint and a brush.

Use actual objects or *LWE Illustrations 3*, pp. 14–15.

1. Teacher models each sentence. Student listens.
2. Teacher models the sentences. Student repeats after each sentence.

Note: Follow the same procedure for all Vocabulary and Structure Focus sections of the lessons from now on.

DRILL: Identification Drill

Teacher holds up an object or points to picture on *LWE Illustrations 3*, p. 16, and asks, "What's this?"

Note: Prompt only when necessary. Review all previous words after each new word.

VOCABULARY: Parts of the Face

Carla has a pretty face.
She has black hair.
She has brown eyes.
She has red lips.
She has pink cheeks.
She has nice teeth.
She has small ears.

Use *LWE Illustrations 3*, p. 16.

DRILL: Identification Drill

Point to different parts of the illustration of the face and ask, "What's this?" Prompt only when necessary.

© New Readers Press. All rights reserved.

STRUCTURE FOCUS: The Use of *shall*

Shall I pick you up after work?	Yes, thank you.
Shall we take the children with us?	No, let's not.
Shall we fix the stairs first?	Yes, let's.
Shall we go away at the end of the month?	Yes, I'd like to.
Shall we have a cup of coffee?	No, not now.
Shall I invite David to come to dinner?	Yes, please do.

Note: The word *Shall* is used with *I* and *we* in polite questions and in questions asking for advice.

DRILL: Making Questions

Teacher gives part of a question.
Student completes the question using *Shall I* or *Shall we*.

Teacher	Student
pick you up after work Shall I pick you up after work?	Shall I pick you up after work?
ask David to come to dinner Shall we ask David to come to dinner?	Shall we ask David to come to dinner?

fix the table
go away at the end of the month
have a cup of coffee
play baseball
watch TV
play cards

DRILL: Answering Questions

Teacher asks a question with *Shall I* or *Shall we*.
Student gives an appropriate affirmative or negative reply.
Encourage the student to use the various replies introduced.

Teacher	Student
Shall I pick you up after work? Yes, thank you.	Yes, thank you.
Shall we have a cup of coffee? No, not now.	No, not now.

Shall we fix the stairs first?
Shall we play cards?
Shall I pick you up after work?
Shall I ask Mrs. King to babysit?
Shall I ask Carla to come to dinner?
Shall we paint the kitchen?

© New Readers Press. All rights reserved.

STRUCTURE FOCUS: *When* Clauses

When Carla calls, I will talk to her.
When the telephone rings, I will answer it.
When the teacher talks, I will listen to her.

Model each sentence, asking the student to listen to *when*.

Note: The *when* clause uses the simple present tense, and the main clause uses *will*.

DRILL: Completion Drill

Teacher gives the *when* clause.
Student completes the sentence using a main clause with *will*.

Teacher	Student
When Carla calls	
When Carla calls, I will talk to her.	When Carla calls, I will talk to her.
When the telephone rings	
When the telephone rings, I will answer it.	When the telephone rings, I will answer it.

When the teacher talks
When David goes to class
When Kay pays her bills
When Gail fixes the chair
When Jason paints the chair
When class starts

© New Readers Press. All rights reserved.

STRUCTURE FOCUS: Verb + Infinitive

	Verb	Infinitive
I'll	learn	to speak English in this class.
I'll	wait	to go home with Kay.
I'll	remember	to get some milk after class.
I'll	ask	to go.

As you model each sentence, have the student listen to *to speak, to go*, and so on.

Note: The verbs used have been introduced previously except for *wait* and *remember*.

DRILL: Completion Drill

Teacher gives the beginning of the sentence, which the student must complete using an infinitive. Student replies may vary.

Teacher	**Student**
I'll ask I'll ask to go.	I'll ask to go.
I'll learn I'll learn to read in this class.	I'll learn to read in this class.

Teacher

I'll need	I'll remember	I'll ask
I'll plan	I'll wait	I'll learn

© New Readers Press. All rights reserved.

STRUCTURE FOCUS: Verb + Object (Noun/Pronoun) + Infinitive

Verb	Object	Infinitive
I'll ask	Carla	to help me.
I'll invite	Kay and Ray	to come with me.
I'll order	them	to go.
I'll teach	them	to read.
I'll tell	them	to stop.
I'll want	him	to help us.

As you model the sentences, explain that *order* means to force someone to do something.

DRILL: Completion Drill

Teacher gives the beginning of the sentence, which the student must complete using a noun or pronoun and an infinitive. Student replies may vary.

Teacher	**Student**
I'll ask I'll ask Carla to call you.	I'll ask Carla to call you.
I'll teach I'll teach them to read.	I'll teach them to read.

Teacher

I'll ask	I'll order	I'll tell	I'll invite
I'll need	I'll teach	I'll want	

DRILL: Completion Drill

Teacher gives the beginning of the sentence, which student must complete by using *to do it* or *you to do it.* (With *want, ask*, and *need*, both answers are correct.)

Teacher	**Student**
I'll learn I'll learn to do it.	I'll learn to do it.
I'll order I'll order you to do it.	I'll order you to do it.

Teacher

I'll teach	I'll plan	I'll want	I'll need	I'll remember
I'll tell	I'll order	I'll ask	I'll learn	I'll wait
				I'll invite

© New Readers Press. All rights reserved.

LISTENING COMPREHENSION

Gail Fisher and Jason Hunt need to buy a hammer and some nails. They are going to fix the kitchen table. After they fix the table, they are going to paint it. They are going to paint the table black.

1. Teacher reads the story twice at a normal pace.
   Student listens. Student asks about words he does not know.
2. Student tells the story in his own words. If the student cannot tell the story, teacher may begin the sentence and have the student complete it.

Note: If the student cannot remember the story, read it once or twice again.

ORAL EVALUATION

1. Using *LWE Illustrations 3*, pp. 14–15, have your student identify basic tools and equipment. He should be able to name 11 items.
2. Using *LWE Illustrations 3*, p. 16, have your student identify parts of the face. He should know all of them.
3. Review *shall* by doing the drills on Making Questions and Answering Questions.
4. Review *when* clauses by doing the Completion Drill.
5. Review the verb + infinitive and verb + object + infinitive by doing the three Completion Drills.

II. Reading and Writing

BOOK 3: Lesson 4

Complete Lesson 4 in book 3, following the instructions given in *Laubach Way to Reading Teacher's Edition 3*. Adapt the wording of the suggested teacher's instructions to the student as needed for your ESL student's comprehension.

ADDITIONAL WRITTEN PRACTICE

After completing Lesson 4 in book 3, have the student do the practices for Lesson 4 in workbook 3.

© New Readers Press. All rights reserved.

Lesson 5

OBJECTIVES

When a student completes this lesson, he should be able to:

1. Say and respond to a new dialog.
2. Say some words about a wedding.
3. Say some words about taking pictures.
4. Say the past participle of the irregular verbs *sing, ring, drink, give, forgive, eat.*
5. Use *already* with the present perfect tense.
6. Use *already* and *yet.*
7. Use *may* for permission.
8. Use reflexive pronouns as objects, as in *I hurt myself.*
9. Use *still* and *any more.*
10. Use verb + gerund, as in *He has quit working.*
11. Listen to a story and repeat it in his own words.

VISUAL AIDS

1. *LWE Illustrations 3*, pp. 17–19.
2. A small pocket mirror.

I. Conversation Skills

DIALOG

A: I'm invited to a lot of parties this month.
B: You are? How many?

A: Three. I'm invited to Jason's birthday party.
I'm invited to a party for Gail before her wedding.
And I'm invited to Jason and Gail's wedding.
B: You'll have to buy three gifts. What are you going to get?

A: I'll get Jason a book. I'll get Gail a pretty nightgown.
I think I'll buy a silver tray for a wedding gift.
B: Sounds very nice. I'm sure they'll like everything.

A: I hope so.

Use the actual objects or *LWE Illustrations 3*, p. 17, for *pretty nightgown* and *silver tray*.

© New Readers Press. All rights reserved.

VOCABULARY: A Wedding

Gail and Jason got married in church.
Many of their friends came to the wedding.
Jason's mother baked a cake for the wedding.
She put the cake on a pretty plate.

Use *LWE Illustrations 3*, p. 18.

DRILL: Identification Drill

Teacher has student identify items by asking, "What's this?" and using the pictures on p. 18 of *LWE Illustrations 3*.

VOCABULARY: Taking Pictures

Gail's uncle has an expensive camera that cost a lot of money.
He buys a lot of film to take pictures with.
When he takes a very good picture, he puts it in a frame.

Use *LWE Illustrations 3*, p. 19.

DRILL: Identification Drill

Teacher has student identify items by asking, "What's this?" and using the pictures on p. 19 of *LWE Illustrations 3*.

VOCABULARY: Past Participles of Irregular Verbs

I sing a song.
I sang a song.
I have sung many songs.

sing	sang	have sung
ring	rang	have rung
drink	drank	have drunk
give	gave	have given
forgive	forgave	have forgiven
eat	ate	have eaten

---

1. Teacher models the first three sentences. Student listens and then repeats.
2. Teacher models all three forms of all the verbs. Student listens.
3. Teacher models all three forms of each verb.
   Student repeats after each set of three verb forms.

© New Readers Press. All rights reserved.

STRUCTURE FOCUS: Present Perfect Tense with *already*

Is she going to sing the song?
She has already sung the song.

Is the bell going to ring?
The bell has already rung.

Are you going to drink some coffee?
I've already drunk some coffee.

Are you going to give her the money?
I've already given her the money.

Are you going to forgive him for what he did?
I've already forgiven him for what he did.

Are you going to eat some cake?
I've already eaten some cake.

1. Teacher models each question and its answer, asking the student to listen to *already*.
   Student listens.

2. Teacher models each question and its answer.
   Student repeats only the answer with *already*.

STRUCTURE FOCUS: The Use of *already* and *yet*

She has already sung the song.
She hasn't sung the song yet.

The bell has already rung.
The bell hasn't rung yet.

I have already drunk some coffee.
I haven't drunk any coffee yet.

1. Teacher models the sentences in pairs with *already* and *yet*, asking the student to listen to *already* and *yet*.
   Student listens.

2. Teacher models the sentences in pairs with *already* and *yet*.
   Student repeats after each sentence.

Note: *Already* is often used in affirmative statements. *Yet* is used in negative statements.

© New Readers Press. All rights reserved.

DRILL: Expansion Drill

Teacher gives a statement to which the student adds *already* or *yet*.

Teacher	Student
She has sung the song. She has already sung the song.	She has already sung the song.
The bell hasn't rung. The bell hasn't rung yet.	The bell hasn't rung yet.

I have drunk some coffee.
I have given her the money.
I haven't forgiven him for what he did.
I have eaten a sandwich.
Jane hasn't sung a song.
The bell hasn't rung.
Carla hasn't drunk any diet soda.
David hasn't given me the book.

DRILL: Answering Questions

Teacher asks student a question which he answers using *already* and the present perfect tense.

Teacher	Student
Is she going to sing the song? She has already sung the song.	She has already sung the song.
Is the bell going to ring? The bell has already rung.	The bell has already rung.

Are you going to drink a diet soda?
Are you going to give her a gift?
Are you going to forgive him for what he said?
Are you going to eat a sandwich?
Is Jane going to sing a song?
Is the bell going to ring?

© New Readers Press. All rights reserved.

STRUCTURE FOCUS: The Use of *may* for Permission

May I have some cake?	Yes, you may.
May I have a sandwich?	Yes, sure.
May I speak to Jane?	Yes, certainly.

Note: *May* is used to ask permission.
The reply *Yes, you may* is more formal than *Sure* or *Certainly.*

DRILL: Making Questions

Teacher gives part of a question. Student completes the question using *May I.*

Teacher	Student
have some cake May I have some cake?	May I have some cake?
speak to David May I speak to David?	May I speak to David?

have a sandwich
use your pen
have some cake
speak to Jane
take your picture
have a drink

DRILL: Answering Questions

Teacher asks a question with *May I,* which student answers with *Yes, you may* or *Sure* or *Certainly.*

Teacher	Student
May I have some cake? Yes, you may.	Yes, you may.
May I speak to Jane? Yes, sure.	Yes, sure.
May I use your pen? Yes, certainly.	Yes, certainly.

May I have a sandwich?
May I speak to David?
May I take your picture?
May I have a drink?
May I use your pen?
May I see your book for a minute?

© New Readers Press. All rights reserved.

STRUCTURE FOCUS: Reflexive Pronouns as Objects

I look at myself in the mirror.
You look at yourself in the mirror.
He looks at himself in the mirror.
She looks at herself in the mirror.
The cat hurt itself.

We look at ourselves in the mirror.
You look at yourselves in the mirror.
They look at themselves in the mirror.

As you model the sentences, ask the student to listen to *myself, yourself,* and so on. Show the student a mirror.

DRILL: Substitution Drill

Teacher gives the subject pronoun.
Student gives the reflexive pronoun that is used with it.

Teacher	Student
I	
myself	myself
you (three people)	
yourselves	yourselves

Teacher

we	she	you (one)	they
he	it	we	you (two people)

DRILL: Answering Questions

Teacher asks questions which student answers using a reflexive pronoun.

Teacher	Student
Who are you talking to?	
I'm talking to myself.	I'm talking to myself.
Who hurt the cat?	
The cat hurt itself.	The cat hurt itself.

Who is Jane talking to?
Who are you reading to?
Who is Carla baking the cake for?
Who are you giving the book to?
Who is David buying the shirt for?
Who are they getting the books for?
Who hurt the cat?

© New Readers Press. All rights reserved.

STRUCTURE FOCUS: The Use of *still* and *any more*

They are still in church.
They aren't in church any more.

Carla is still at home.
Carla isn't at home any more.

As you model the sentences, ask the student to listen to *still* and *any more*.

Note: *Still* is used in affirmative statements.
Any more is used in negative statements.

DRILL: Expansion Drill

Teacher gives a sentence to which the student adds *still* or *any more*.

Teacher	**Student**
He is at home. He is still at home.	He is still at home.
He isn't at home. He isn't at home any more.	He isn't at home any more.
We see Gail at work. We don't see Gail at work.	
They live in New York. They don't live in New York.	
I have my car. I don't have my car.	
She works at the paper factory. She doesn't work at the paper factory.	

© New Readers Press. All rights reserved.

STRUCTURE FOCUS: Verb + Gerund

	Verb	Gerund
I've	finished	reading the book.
I've	stopped	talking to her.
He has	quit	working.

As you model the sentences, ask the student to listen to *reading, talking,* and *working*.

Note: The verbs *quit* and *finish* are new here.

DRILL: Completion Drill

Teacher gives the beginning of a sentence which student must complete using a gerund. Student replies may vary.

Teacher	Student
I've finished I've finished reading the book.	I've finished reading the book.
He has quit He has quit working.	He has quit working.
I've stopped He has quit He has practiced They have stopped We have finished	

LISTENING COMPREHENSION

Ed and Jane went to a wedding. First, they went to the church to see the wedding. After the wedding, they went to the wedding party.

At the party, there was a big wedding cake, sandwiches, coffee, and other drinks. Ed helped himself to a sandwich and coffee. Jane helped herself to a piece of the wedding cake.

1. Teacher reads the story twice at a normal pace.
   Student listens. Student asks about words he does not know.

2. Student tells the story in his own words. If the student cannot tell the story, teacher may begin the sentence and have the student complete it.

Note: If the student cannot remember the story, read it once or twice again.

© New Readers Press. All rights reserved.

ORAL EVALUATION

1. Using *LWE Illustrations 3*, p. 18, have the student identify the words about a wedding. Student should know all of them.
2. Using *LWE Illustrations 3*, p. 19, have the student identify the words about taking pictures. Student should know all of them.
3. Have the student say the past and past participle of the irregular verbs and use them with *already* in the present perfect tense. Student should know all of them.
4. Review *already* and *yet* by doing the Expansion Drill.
5. Review the use of *may* for permission by doing the drills on Making Questions and Answering Questions.
6. Review the use of the reflexive pronouns as objects by doing the drill on Answering Questions.
7. Review the use of *still* and *any more* by doing the Expansion Drill.
8. Review the use of verb + gerund by doing the Completion Drill.

II. Reading and Writing

BOOK 3: Lesson 5

Complete Lesson 5 in book 3, following the instructions given in *Laubach Way to Reading Teacher's Edition 3*. Adapt the wording of the suggested teacher's instructions to the student as needed for your ESL student's comprehension.

ADDITIONAL WRITTEN PRACTICE

After completing Lesson 5 in book 3, have the student do the practices for Lesson 5 in workbook 3.

© New Readers Press. All rights reserved.

Lesson 6

OBJECTIVES

When a student completes this lesson, he should be able to:

1. Say and respond to a new dialog.
2. Use some idioms with *take, do*, and *make*.
3. Say some vocabulary concerning items of personal grooming.
4. Use *by* + reflexive pronouns, as in *I live by myself.*
5. Use the past progressive tense.
6. Use infinitives and gerunds.
7. Listen to a story and repeat it in his own words.

VISUAL AIDS

1. *LWE Illustrations 3*, pp. 20–23.
2. Any of these items you can bring:

washcloth	soap	toothbrush	shampoo	comb
towel	razor	toothpaste	hairdryer	hairbrush

I. Conversation Skills

DIALOG

A: Where were you going when I saw you yesterday?
B: I was going to the movies.

A: Do you always go to the movies by yourself?
B: Sometimes I go alone, and sometimes I go with friends.

A: I'd like to go with you sometime.
B: That's a good idea. I'll call you.

© New Readers Press. All rights reserved.

VOCABULARY: Idioms with *do*, *make*, and *take*

do

Jason always does a good job.
Jason does the dishes.
Gail does the laundry.

make

Ray makes a good cup of coffee.
David makes good cakes.
Carla makes dinner for Rosa and herself.

take

I take a walk every day.
I take a shower or a bath every morning.
I take my lunch to work every day.

Model the sentences, asking the student to listen to *does*, *makes*, and *take*. Use *LWE Illustrations 3*, p. 20, for *shower* and *bath*, which are new here.

Note: These are idiomatic expressions which the student must learn.

DRILL: Making Sentences

Teacher gives the student a word or phrase which student uses in a sentence with *do, make*, or *take*.

Teacher	Student
a good job Jason always does a good job.	Jason always does a good job.
a walk I take a walk every night.	I take a walk every night.
a shower in the morning	
the dishes	
my lunch to work	
breakfast before I go to work	
good cakes	
a cup of coffee	
a walk every morning	
a bath in the evening	

© New Readers Press. All rights reserved.

VOCABULARY: Items of Personal Grooming

I wash my hands with soap.
I wash my face with a washcloth.
I dry my hands and face with a towel.
I brush my teeth with a toothbrush and toothpaste.
I shave with a razor.
I wash my hair with shampoo.
I dry my hair with a hairdryer.
I comb my hair with a comb.
I brush my hair with a hairbrush.

Use actual objects or *LWE Illustrations 3*, pp. 21–23.

DRILL: Question and Answer Drill

Teacher asks questions to elicit vocabulary items.

Teacher	**Student**
How do you brush your hair? With a hairbrush.	With a hairbrush.
How do you comb your hair? With a comb.	With a comb.

How do you wash your hands?
How do you dry your face?
How do you brush your teeth?
How do you shave?
How do you wash your hair?
How do you dry your hair?
How do you brush your hair?
How do you comb your hair?

© New Readers Press. All rights reserved.

STRUCTURE FOCUS: *by* + Reflexive Pronouns

Do you live alone?	Yes, I live by myself.
Does Jane live alone?	Yes, she lives by herself.
Does David go to work alone?	Yes, he goes by himself.

As you model the sentences, ask the student to listen to *by myself, by herself,* and *by himself.*

DRILL: Answering Questions

Teacher asks questions using the word *alone*.
Student answers using *by* and a reflexive pronoun. Student replies may vary.

Teacher	**Student**
Does Jane live alone? Yes, she lives by herself.	Yes, she lives by herself.
Do you like to go shopping alone? No, I don't like to go by myself.	No, I don't like to go by myself.

Do you live alone?
Does Ann like to go shopping alone?
Do you go to class alone?
Do they go swimming alone?
Does David like to go to the movies alone?
Do you go fishing alone?

© New Readers Press. All rights reserved.

STRUCTURE FOCUS: Past Progressive Tense

He <u>was</u> <u>sleeping</u> when I called him last night.
I <u>was</u> <u>reading</u> a book when they called yesterday.
We <u>were</u> <u>watching</u> TV when you called.

As you model the sentences, ask the student to listen to *was sleeping, was reading*, and *were watching*.

Note: The past progressive tense is used for an action in progress at a particular time in the past.

DRILL: Answering Questions

Teacher asks questions which the student answers using the past progressive tense.

Teacher	**Student**
What was Lee doing when you called him last night? sleeping He was sleeping when I called him last night.	 He was sleeping when I called him last night.
What was Jane reading when you called her yesterday? a book She was reading a book when I called her yesterday.	 She was reading a book when I called her yesterday.

Teacher

What were you doing when they called yesterday?
studying

What was she doing when Rosa went to sleep?
singing to Rosa

What were you doing when you had the accident?
driving my car

What was she wearing when you saw her?
a red dress

What was Lee doing when you called him?
eating dinner

© New Readers Press. All rights reserved.

STRUCTURE FOCUS: Review of Infinitive and Gerund

I'll learn	to speak	English in this class.
I'll tell him	to read	the book.
I'll finish	reading	the book.
He has quit	working.	

As you model the sentences, ask the student to listen to *to speak, to read, reading*, and *working*.

DRILL: Completion Drill

Teacher begins a sentence which student completes with either *to do it* or *doing it*.

Teacher	**Student**
I'll wait I'll wait to do it.	I'll wait to do it.
I have finished I have finished doing it.	I have finished doing it.

Teacher

I'll learn	I'll need	I'll plan	I'll wait	She'll stop
I'll keep	I'll quit	I'll remember	He'll practice	They'll finish

LISTENING COMPREHENSION

Many people have cameras. They take pictures of their family and their friends. They take pictures of trees and rivers. They put the pictures in a book. Then they show the pictures to their family and friends.

1. Teacher reads the story twice at a normal pace.
   Student listens. Student asks about words he does not know.
2. Student tells the story in his own words. If the student cannot tell the story, teacher may begin the sentence and have the student complete it.

Note: If the student cannot remember the story, read it once or twice again.

© New Readers Press. All rights reserved.

ORAL EVALUATION

1. Using *LWE Illustrations 3*, p. 20, review idioms with *do, make*, and *take* by doing the drill on Making Sentences. Student should know all the idioms.
2. Using *LWE Illustrations 3*, pp. 21–23, review items of personal grooming. Students should know 7 of them.
3. Review the use of *by* + reflexive pronouns by doing the Answering Questions Drill.
4. Review the past progressive tense by doing the Answering Questions Drill.
5. Review the use of the infinitive and the gerund by doing the Completion Drill.

II. Reading and Writing

BOOK 3: Lesson 6

Complete Lesson 6 in book 3, following the instructions given in *Laubach Way to Reading Teacher's Edition 3*. Adapt the wording of the suggested teacher's instructions to the student as needed for your ESL student's comprehension.

ADDITIONAL WRITTEN PRACTICE

After completing Lesson 6 in book 3, have the student do the practices for Lesson 6 in workbook 3.

© New Readers Press. All rights reserved.

Lesson 7

OBJECTIVES

When a student completes this lesson, he should be able to:

1. Say and respond to a new dialog.
2. Say some words about beverages.
3. Say some words concerning the outdoors.
4. Say some adjectives about feelings.
5. Say some adjectives that are opposites.
6. Say some vocabulary about the inside of a car.
7. Use the word *again.*
8. Use the irregular verbs *sleep, keep, feel, sweep, mean, send, spend,* and their past participles.
9. Use *am, is, are, was*, and *were* for emphasis.
10. Use *do*, *does*, and *did* for emphasis.
11. Listen to numbers and write them down.

VISUAL AIDS

1. *LWE Illustrations 3*, pp. 24–26.
2. Some ads for used cars from the newspaper.

I. Conversation Skills

DIALOG

A: I'd like to buy a car.
B: Cars are expensive. What kind are you going to get?

A: A small used car. One that gets good gas mileage.
B: That's a good idea.
Maybe you'll find some ads for used cars in today's newspaper.
Let's look.

A: OK.

Use *LWE Illustrations 3*, p. 24.
Also, show some used car ads from the newspaper.

© New Readers Press. All rights reserved.

VOCABULARY: Beverages

When it's hot, a person likes to have a cold drink.
Some people drink water or soda with ice in it.
Some people drink iced tea or iced coffee.
Some people drink cold beer.
Some people drink wine.

Use *LWE Illustrations 3,* p. 25.

DRILL: Identification Drill

Teacher asks a question (such as "What do some people drink when it's hot?"), pointing to the illustrations on p. 25 of *LWE Illustrations 3.*

Note: Review all previous words after each new word.

DRILL: Answering Questions

Teacher asks questions which elicit vocabulary items about beverages. Student must give a different answer each time.

Teacher	**Student**
What do some people like to drink?	
iced tea	
Some people like to drink iced tea.	Some people like to drink iced tea.
What do you like to drink?	
etc.	

© New Readers Press. All rights reserved.

VOCABULARY: The Outdoors

I like to go camping.
I like to be outdoors.
I like the green trees and the blue sky.
I like the fresh air.

Use *LWE Illustrations 3*, p. 24. You can color the trees green and the sky blue before class.

DRILL: Identification

Teacher asks a question about the vocabulary having to do with the outdoors, pointing to the appropriate illustration on p. 24 of *LWE Illustrations 3*.

Note: Review all previous words after each new word.

VOCABULARY: Adjectives about Feelings

We feel angry when a friend yells at us.
We feel sad when a friend is sick.
We feel glad when a friend gets better.
Mrs. Green feels upset when her son comes home very late.

Pantomime the meaning of the adjectives.

DRILL: Question and Answer Drill

Teacher asks questions to elicit vocabulary items.

Teacher	Student
How do we feel when a friend yells at us? We feel angry.	We feel angry.
How do we feel when a friend is sick? We feel sad.	We feel sad.
How do we feel when a friend gets better? How do we feel when a friend yells at us? How do we feel when a friend is sick? How does Mrs. Green feel when her son comes home late?	

© New Readers Press. All rights reserved.

VOCABULARY: Adjective Opposites

The book is open.
The book is shut.

Beans are cheap.
Meat is expensive.

The day is bright.
The night is dark.

The big building is high.
The small building is low.

He's working in the garden. His hands are dirty.
He washes his hands. His hands are clean.

---

1. Teacher models each word in pairs of sentences, giving the opposites. Explain the words the student doesn't understand. Student listens.
2. Teacher models the pairs of sentences. Student repeats each pair of sentences.

DRILL: Question and Answer Drill

Teacher asks student to give vocabulary items.

Teacher	**Student**
Tell about the book. The book is open.	The book is open.
Tell about beans. Beans are cheap.	Beans are cheap.

Tell about meat.
Tell about beans.
Tell about the day.
Tell about the night.
Tell about the big building.
Tell about the small building.
Tell about the book. (Open the book.)
Tell about the book. (Shut the book.)
Tell about your hands when you wash them.
Tell about your hands when you work in the garden.

© New Readers Press. All rights reserved.

VOCABULARY: Inside the Car

Inside the car there is a steering wheel.
There is a front seat and a back seat.
The driver sits on the front seat behind the wheel.
The passenger sits in the passenger's side in the front seat.
Passengers sit in the back seat.

Use *LWE Illustrations 3*, p. 26.

DRILL: Question and Answer Drill

Teacher asks questions to elicit vocabulary items.

Teacher	**Student**
Where does the driver sit?	
The driver sits in the front seat behind the wheel.	The driver sits in the front seat behind the wheel.
Where does the passenger sit?	
The passenger sits on the passenger's side in the front seat.	The passenger sits on the passenger's side in the front seat.

Who sits in the back seat?
Where is the steering wheel?
Where does the driver sit?
Where do the passengers sit?

© New Readers Press. All rights reserved.

VOCABULARY: The Use of *again*

> The plate isn't clean. Wash it again.
> I didn't understand the story. Read it again.

As you model each pair of sentences, ask the student to listen to *again*.

DRILL: Rejoinder Drill

Teacher makes a statement, to which the student replies using the imperative and *again*.

Teacher	**Student**
The plates aren't clean. Wash them again.	Wash them again.
I don't understand this story. Read it again.	Read it again.
The cups are still dirty.	
The knives are still dirty.	
I can't say this word.	
I don't understand this story.	

VOCABULARY: Irregular Verbs

> I sleep very well at night.
> I feel fine.
> He keeps his wallet in his pocket.
> I sweep the floor every day.
> He means a lot to me.
> I send my mother a letter every week.
> I spend a lot of money every week.

Pantomime the meaning of the verbs if an explanation is necessary.

© New Readers Press. All rights reserved.

VOCABULARY: Past Participles of Irregular Verbs

sleep	slept	have slept
keep	kept	have kept
feel	felt	have felt
sweep	swept	have swept
mean	meant	have meant
send	sent	have sent
spend	spent	have spent

Teacher models all three forms of each verb. Student repeats.

DRILL: Answering Questions

1. Teacher asks a question in the present perfect tense which the student answers in the negative.
2. Teacher models first two items. Student listens.

Teacher	**Student**
Have you slept well this week? No, I haven't slept well this week.	No, I haven't slept well this week.
Have you kept on working? No, I haven't kept on working.	No, I haven't kept on working.

Have you felt well this week?
Have you swept the floor yet?
Have you ever slept in a tent?
Have you meant what you said?
Have you sent Jane a letter yet?
Have you spent all your money yet?

© New Readers Press. All rights reserved.

STRUCTURE FOCUS: The Use of *am, is, are* for Emphasis

You aren't Spanish.	Yes,	I am Spanish.
He isn't married.	Yes,	he is married.
They aren't home.	Yes,	they are home.
It wasn't fun.	Yes,	it was fun.
She wasn't in bed.	Yes,	she was in bed.
They weren't in the kitchen.	Yes,	they were in the kitchen.

1. Teacher models the negative sentence and the emphatic sentence in pairs. Have the student listen to the emphatic form of the verb. Student listens.
2. Teacher models the sentences, stressing the verb *be* (*am, is, are, was, were*). Student repeats, also stressing the verb.

Note: The forms of the verb *be* are stressed in a sentence to emphasize the point being made and often to contradict something that has been said.

DRILL: Rejoinder Drill

Teacher makes a statement in the negative which student contradicts by making an affirmative statement, stressing the verb *be*.

Teacher	**Student**
You aren't Cuban. Yes, I *am* Cuban.	Yes, I *am* Cuban.
Ray isn't married to Kay. Yes, he *is* married to Kay.	Yes, he *is* married to Kay.

Rosa isn't a baby.
They aren't home.
It wasn't fun.
The babysitter wasn't taking care of Rosa.
Kay isn't paying her bills.
They weren't playing basketball.

© New Readers Press. All rights reserved.

Structure Focus: The Use of *do* for Emphasis

You don't study English.	Yes,	I do study English.
You don't live in ___________.	Yes,	I do live in ___________.
He doesn't speak English.	Yes,	he does speak English.
You didn't come to class last week.	Yes,	I did come to class last week.
Kay didn't pay the rent.	Yes,	Kay did pay the rent.
Ray didn't bake the cake.	Yes,	Ray did bake the cake.

1. Teacher models the negative sentence and the emphatic affirmative sentence in pairs. Have the student listen to the emphatic form of the verb.
2. Teacher models each pair of sentences, stressing the verb *do* in the emphatic sentence. Student repeats the emphatic sentence, also stressing the verb.

Note: The verb *do* is used for emphasis. Be sure the student stresses *do* and *did* as he imitates the teacher.

DRILL: Rejoinder Drill

1. Teacher makes a statement in the negative which student contradicts by making an affirmative sentence using *do* or *did.*
2. Teacher models first two items. Student listens.

Teacher	**Student**
You don't study English. Yes, I *do* study English.	Yes, I *do* study English.
Ray didn't bake the cake. Yes, Ray *did* bake the cake.	Yes, Ray *did* bake the cake.

You don't live on ___________ Street.
Jason didn't fix the stairs.
You don't study English.
Kay and Ray didn't go away.
They don't like to go camping.
Kay didn't pay her bills.
You didn't come to class yesterday.

PRONUNCIATION AND LISTENING COMPREHENSION

1. Teacher says the numbers from 1 to 100 in groups of 10. Student listens.
2. Teacher models the numbers in groups of 10. Student repeats. Help the student with numbers he has difficulty with, such as the difference between 13 and 30, 14 and 40 and so on.

© New Readers Press. All rights reserved.

DRILL: Listening Comprehension

Teacher says the number. The student writes the number he hears on a piece of paper on the blackboard. Do not emphasize the endings (*-ty, -teen*). Read the numbers across, that is 3–13–30 and so on.

3	13	30
4	14	40
5	15	50
6	16	60
7	17	70
8	18	80
9	19	90

Do the numbers again in a different order; for example, say 13–6–9 and so on.

ORAL EVALUATION

1. Using *LWE Illustrations 3*, p. 25, have the student identify the beverages. He should know 3 of them.
2. Using *LWE Illustrations 3*, p. 24, have the student review terms about the outdoors. He should know all of them.
3. Review adjectives about feelings by doing the Question and Answer Drill. Student should know all of them.
4. Review adjective opposites by doing the Question and Answer Drill. Student should know all of them.
5. Review terms about inside the car by doing the Question and Answer Drill. Student should know all of them.
6. Review irregular verbs by doing the drill on Answering Questions. Student should know all of them.
7. Review *am, is, are* for emphasis by doing the Rejoinder Drill.
8. Review *do* for emphasis by doing the Rejoinder Drill.

II. Reading and Writing

BOOK 3: Lesson 7

Complete Lesson 7 in book 3, following the instructions given in *Laubach Way to Reading Teacher's Edition 3*. Adapt the wording of the suggested teacher's instructions to the student as needed for your ESL student's comprehension.

ADDITIONAL WRITTEN PRACTICE

After completing Lesson 7 in book 3, have the student do the practices for Lesson 7 in workbook 3.

© New Readers Press. All rights reserved.

Lesson 8

OBJECTIVES

When a student completes this lesson, he should be able to:

1. Say and respond to a new dialog.
2. Say some prepositions.
3. Say some names of fruit.
4. Use indefinite pronouns: *everything, something, nothing, anything.*
5. Use indefinite pronouns: *everyone, someone, no one, anyone.*
6. Use *each.*
7. Use *best* and *worst* with the present prefect tense.
8. Listen to a story and repeat it in his own words.

VISUAL AIDS

1. *LWE Illustrations 3*, pp. 27–29.
2. Any of the following fruits that it is convenient to bring, or color pictures of them.

apple	bananas	grapes	lemon
pear	orange	peach	watermelon

I. Conversation Skills

DIALOG

A: Food is getting more expensive every day.
B: That's true.
I can't afford to buy meat very often.

A: I know. We can't either.
We eat a lot of beans and rice.
B: We do, too.

1. Model the entire dialog two or three times. Student listens.
2. Model each line. Student repeats after each line.
3. Teacher takes one role of the dialog. Student takes the other.
4. Reverse roles.

© New Readers Press. All rights reserved.

VOCABULARY: Prepositions of Location

Ray is sitting between Kay and Carla.
Carla is sitting next to Ray.
David is sitting in back of Carla.
Jason is sitting in front of Carla.
The teacher is in the front of the room.
The coats are in the back of the room.

Use *LWE Illustrations 3*, p. 27, to show the meaning of each preposition.

DRILL: Answering Questions

Depending on the number of people in the room, the teacher can move around, placing herself *between* two students, *next to* a student, *in back of* one and *in front of* one. She may stand *in the front of* the room and *in the back of* the room. As the teacher stands in different positions, she asks questions like "Who am I standing between?" and "Where am I?" to elicit the prepositions being taught.

VOCABULARY: Fruit

Many people eat fruit.
They eat apples.
They eat pears.
They eat bananas.
They eat oranges.
They eat grapes.
They eat watermelons.
They eat peaches.
They eat lemons.

Use *LWE Illustrations 3*, pp. 28–29, or actual objects, or color pictures of fruit.

Note: You may wish to add other fruits, depending on what foods are part of your student's diet, for example, pineapple, grapefruit, or cherries.

DRILL: Identification Drill

Teacher points to the illustrations on pp. 28–29 of *LWE Illustrations 3* and asks, "What do people eat?"

© New Readers Press. All rights reserved.

STRUCTURE FOCUS: Indefinite Pronouns with *-thing*

Everything is on the table.
Something is on the table.
Nothing is on the table.
There isn't anything on the table.

As you model each sentence, ask the student to listen to *everything, something, nothing*, and *anything*.

Note: The words *everything, something, nothing*, and *anything* are indefinite pronouns. They take a singular verb.

DRILL: Making Sentences

Teacher uses one indefinite pronoun in a sentence and asks the student to substitute the other indefinite pronouns in the same sentence or a similar one.

Teacher	**Student**
Everything is here.	
nothing	
Nothing is here.	Nothing is here.
anything	
There isn't anything here.	There isn't anything here.
Everything is on the desk.	
something	
nothing	
anything	
Everything looks nice.	
something	
nothing	
I see everything in the room.	
something	
nothing	
anything	

© New Readers Press. All rights reserved.

STRUCTURE FOCUS: Indefinite Pronouns with -*one*

Everyone is here.
Someone is here.
No one is here.
There isn't anyone here.

As you model each sentence, ask the student to listen to *everyone, someone, no one*, and *anyone*. Explain that these words refer to persons.

Note: The words *everyone, someone, no one*, and *anyone* are indefinite pronouns that refer to a person or persons. They take a singular verb. In informal usage, we say, "Everyone must hand in their papers." In formal usage, we say, "Everyone must hand in his paper."

DRILL: Making Sentences

Teacher uses one indefinite pronoun in a sentence and asks the student to substitute the other indefinite pronouns in the same sentence or a similar one.

Teacher	Student
Everyone is in the room.	
someone	
Someone is in the room.	Someone is in the room.
no one	
No one is in the room.	No one is in the room.
anyone	
There isn't anyone in the room.	There isn't anyone in the room.

I see everyone in the room.
someone
no one
anyone

I will give everyone a gift.
someone
no one
anyone

Everyone knows the answer.
someone
no one

© New Readers Press. All rights reserved.

STRUCTURE FOCUS: The Use of *each*

Each book is the same.
Each person brings something to the party.

As you model each sentence, ask the student to listen to *each*.

Note: *Each* takes a singular verb.

DRILL: Making Sentences

Teacher makes a sentence about everyone in the class.
Student makes a similar sentence using *each*.

Teacher	**Student**
Everyone in the class has a book. each book Each book is the same.	Each book is the same.
Everyone in the class has a car. each car Each car is not the same.	Each car is not the same.
Everyone in the class has a name. each name	
Everyone in the class is wearing a ring. each ring	
Everyone in the class has a book. each book	
Everyone in the class has a camera. each camera	
Everyone in the class has a pen. each pen	

© New Readers Press. All rights reserved.

STRUCTURE FOCUS: The Present Perfect Tense with *best* and *worst*

This is the best sandwich I have ever eaten.
This is the best party we have ever had.
This is the worst music I have ever listened to.
This is the worst meat I have ever eaten.

As you model each sentence, ask the student to listen to *the best* or the *worst.*

Note: Explain that *best* is used for something very good, while *worst* is used for something very bad. (It is not necessary at this time to teach *good, better, best* and *bad, worse, worst.*)

DRILL: Completion Drill

Teacher begins a sentence containing *best* or *worst*, which the student completes using the present perfect tense.

Teacher	Student
This is the best sandwich	
This is the best sandwich I have ever eaten.	This is the best sandwich I have ever eaten.
This is the worst cake.	
This is the worst cake I have ever eaten.	This is the worst cake I have ever eaten.
This is the best party	
This is the worst meat	
You are the best friend	
These are the worst beans	
This is the best music	

LISTENING COMPREHENSION

Carla's class had a dinner party. There were eighteen people at the party. They had meat, beans, baked potatoes, and a green salad. They had tea, coffee, apples, and cheese. They had fun eating a big meal together.

---

1. Teacher reads the story twice at a normal pace.
   Student listens. Student asks about words he does not know.
2. Student tells the story in his own words. If the student cannot tell the story, teacher may begin the sentence and have the student complete it.

Note: If the student cannot remember the story, read it once or twice again.

© New Readers Press. All rights reserved.

ORAL EVALUATION

1. Review prepositions of location by doing the drill on Answering Questions. Student should know all the prepositions.
2. Using *LWE Illustrations 3*, pp. 28–29, have the student identify the names of the fruits. Student should know 7 of them.
3. Review the indefinite pronouns with *-thing* and *-one* by doing the two drills on Making Sentences.
4. Review *each* by doing the drill on Making Sentences.
5. Review the use of *best* and *worst* with the present perfect tense by doing the Completion Drill.

II. Reading and Writing

BOOK 3: Lesson 8

Complete Lesson 8 in book 3, following the instructions given in *Laubach Way to Reading Teacher's Edition 3*. Adapt the wording of the suggested teacher's instructions to the student as necessary for the comprehension of your ESL student.

ADDITIONAL WRITTEN PRACTICE

After completing Lesson 8 in book 3, have the student do the practices for Lesson 8 in workbook 3.

© New Readers Press. All rights reserved.

Lesson 9

OBJECTIVES

When a student completes this lesson, he should be able to:

1. Say and respond to a new dialog.
2. Say words concerning a repair bill: *repair, parts, labor, tax.*
3. Say some words concerning items used for cleaning.
4. Say the chart word *key.*
5. Say some words about saving money.
6. Say the ordinal numbers: *first* to *one hundredth.*
7. Use the past *be* + *going to.*
8. Use adjective clauses with *that.*
9. Listen to a story and repeat it in his own words.

VISUAL AIDS

1. *LWE Illustrations 3*, pp. 30–31.
2. Keys on a chain.

I. Conversation Skills

DIALOG

Steve:	May I help you?
Mrs. Green:	Yes, I'd like to have my radio fixed.
Steve:	What's wrong with it?
Mrs. Green:	I don't know. It doesn't work.
Steve:	We'll look it over and try to fix it.
Mrs. Green:	When will it be ready?
Steve:	In a week. Here's your ticket for the radio.
Mrs. Green:	Thank you.

Vary the dialog by practicing with other items to be repaired that the student may suggest.

© New Readers Press. All rights reserved.

VOCABULARY: A Repair Bill

Jane Fisher's TV was not working.
She asked Pete to fix her TV. Pete has a *repair* shop.
Jane's TV repair cost $12.14 for new *parts*.
Her TV repair cost $30.00 for the *labor* Peter did to fix the TV.
The *sales tax* on her bill was $2.53.

Note: Explain that *repair* means "fix" and that *parts* for a TV could be a new knob or picture tube. "Labor" is the work involved. Discuss the local sales tax student must pay in his community.

DRILL: Answering Questions

Teacher asks questions to elicit vocabulary items.

Teacher	Student
Was Jane Fisher's TV working? No, her TV wasn't working.	No, her TV wasn't working.
Why did she ask Pete to fix her TV? Pete had a repair shop.	Pete had a repair shop.
What did Jane pay $12.14 for? What did Jane pay $30.00 for? What did Jane pay $2.53 for? How much is the sales tax where you live?	

© New Readers Press. All rights reserved.

VOCABULARY: Items Used for Cleaning

When Steve cleans the shop, he uses many things.
He sweeps the floor with a broom.
He picks up the dirt with a dustpan.
He washes the floor with a mop.
He vacuums the rug with a vacuum cleaner.
He puts soap and water in a pail and washes the windows with a sponge.
He puts old paper and dirt in a trash can.

Use *LWE Illustrations 3,* pp. 30–31.

DRILL: Question and Answer Drill

Teacher asks questions to elicit vocabulary items.

Teacher	Student
What does Steve sweep the floor with? A broom.	A broom.
What does he pick the dirt up with? A dustpan.	A dustpan.
What does Steve wash the floor with? What does he sweep the floor with? What does he vacuum the rug with? Where does he put soap and water? Where does he put the old paper and dirt? What does he pick the dirt up with?	

VOCABULARY: Kinds of Keys

I have a lot of keys.
I keep my keys on a key chain.
I have a house key.
I have a car key.
I have a key to my bicycle lock.

VOCABULARY: Saving Money

Every week I spend money on food and rent.
Every week I save some money.
I save the money in the bank.
I put my money in a savings account.
I want to save money to buy many things.

© New Readers Press. All rights reserved.

VOCABULARY: Ordinal Numbers

first	eleventh	tenth
second	twelfth	twentieth
third	thirteenth	thirtieth
fourth	fourteenth	fortieth
fifth	fifteenth	fiftieth
sixth	sixteenth	sixtieth
seventh	seventeenth	seventieth
eighth	eighteenth	eightieth
ninth	nineteenth	nintieth
tenth	twentieth	one hundredth

1. Teacher models the ordinal numbers in groups of five, going down each column here. (In the last column, when you are counting by 10s, start again at *tenth*.)
2. Teacher models the numbers. Student repeats after each number.

DRILL: Saying Ordinal Numbers

1. Teacher writes a number on the board and says the number. Student repeats.
2. Teacher writes a number on the board. Student says the number.
3. Reverse roles. Have the student say the numbers as the teacher writes the numbers on the board.

Note: Help the student with his pronunciation if necessary.

© New Readers Press. All rights reserved.

VOCABULARY: Using Ordinal Numbers in Sentences

We went to Snake River for three days.
The first day we went swimming.
The second day we went fishing.
The third day we had a picnic.

---

1. Teacher models each number in a sentence. Student listens.
2. Teacher models the sentences. Student repeats after each sentence.

DRILL: Answering Questions

Teacher asks questions which elicit the ordinal numbers in the student's answers.

Teacher	Student
When did you go swimming at Snake River? We went swimming the first day.	We went swimming the first day.
When did you go fishing at Snake River? We went fishing the second day.	We went fishing the second day.

When did you go swimming at Snake River?
When did you go fishing at Snake River?
When did you go on a picnic at Snake River?
What is the first thing you do when you come to class?
What is the first thing you do when you get up in the morning?

© New Readers Press. All rights reserved.

STRUCTURE FOCUS: Past of *be* + *going to*

I was going to buy the watch, but I didn't.
We were going to go home at 7 o'clock, but we didn't.
They were going to buy a car, but they didn't.

As you model each sentence, ask the student to listen to *was going to* and *were going to.*

Note: The form *be* in the past + *going to* is used to express a past intention that may not have been carried out.

DRILL: Answering Questions

Teacher asks questions which student answers using the past of *be* + *going* + infinitive.

Teacher	**Student**
What were you going to do before class? I was going to study but I didn't.	I was going to study but I didn't.
What was Jason going to do first? He was going to paint the stairs first.	He was going to paint the stairs first.
What was Carla going to bake? Which bill was Kay going to pay? What were you going to buy? Where were you going to go after class? When were you going to have a party? What was Pete going to do?	

© New Readers Press. All rights reserved.

STRUCTURE FOCUS: Adjective Clauses with *that*

Steve gave Mrs. Green the radio that he fixed.
I like the frame that Gail put her picture in.
You can keep the money that Mrs. Green gave you.

As you model each sentence, ask the student to listen to *that*.

DRILL: Combining Sentences

Teacher gives two sentences which the student combines using an adjective clause with *that*.

Teacher	Student
Steve gave Mrs. Green the radio. He fixed the radio. Steve gave Mrs. Green the radio that he fixed.	Steve gave Mrs. Green the radio that he fixed.
I like the frame. Gail put her picture in the frame. I like the frame that Gail put her picture in.	I like the frame that Gail put her picture in.
You can keep the money. Mrs. Green gave you the money.	
Ms. Smith brings the meat. Each person helped to pay for the meat.	
They painted the apartment. They live in the apartment.	
Mrs. King is a lady. I like her a lot.	
They cut the wedding cake. Jason's mother baked the cake.	
Lee Green went to see the tree. He hit the tree.	
At the party they had the beans. Carla made the beans.	

© New Readers Press. All rights reserved.

LISTING COMPREHENSION

I was going to listen to my radio, but it wasn't working. I took the radio to the Valley Repair Shop. I asked Pete to fix my radio. He said he was very busy. He needed a week to fix my radio. I was sorry. I need my radio. I listen to music and the news on the radio every morning and every night.

1. Teacher reads the story twice at a normal pace.
   Student listens. Student asks about words he does not know.
2. Student tells the story in his own words. If the student cannot tell the story, teacher may begin the sentence and have the student complete it.

Note: If the student cannot remember the story, read it once or twice again.

ORAL EVALUATION

1. Review the words concerning a repair bill by doing the drill on Answering Questions. Student should know all the items.
2. Using *LWE Illustrations 3*, pp. 30–31, review words on items used for cleaning by doing the Question and Answer Drill. Student should know 5 of the items.
3. Review words about saving money. Student should know all the words.
4. Review the ordinal numbers by doing the drill on Saying Ordinal Numbers.
5. Review the past of *be* + *going to* by doing the drill on Answering Questions.
6. Review adjective clauses with *that* by doing the drill on Combining Sentences.

II. Reading and Writing

BOOK 3: Lesson 9

Complete Lesson 9 in book 3, following the instructions given in *Laubach Way to Reading Teacher's Edition 3*. Adapt the wording of the suggested teacher's instructions to the student as necessary for the comprehension of your ESL student.

ADDITIONAL WRITTEN PRACTICE

After completing Lesson 9 in book 3, have the student do the practices for Lesson 9 in workbook 3.

© New Readers Press. All rights reserved.

Lesson 10

OBJECTIVES

When a student completes this lesson, he should be able to:

1. Say and respond to a new dialog.
2. Say some words about the stages of life.
3. Say some story words: *Canada*, *the United States, country, city*, and *state*.
4. Use some idioms with *take* and *make*.
5. Use *more ... than* with nouns.
6. Use question words + infinitives.
7. Listen to a story and repeat it in his own words.

VISUAL AIDS

LWE Illustrations 3, pp. 32–33.

I. Conversation Skills

DIALOG

A: I really like your new car.
B: Thanks. I do, too.

A: When did you get it?
B: About three weeks ago.

A: How does it run?
B: Great. It's a nice car.

VOCABULARY: Stages of Life

An infant is a baby.
A child is a very young person.
A teenager is anyone from the age of 13 to 19.
An adult is anyone over 21 years old.

Use *LWE Illustrations 3*, p. 32.

DRILL: Identification Drill

Teacher asks, "Who's this?" as she points to the various people on p. 32 of *LWE Illustrations 3*.

© New Readers Press. All rights reserved.

VOCABULARY: Canada and the United States

Canada and the United States are big countries.
Canada is a neighbor of the United States.
The United States has fifty states.
It has many, many cities.
Ann Baker lives in the city of Dallas, in the state of Texas.

---

1. Use *LWE Illustrations 3*, p. 33. On that map, write in the names of the student's city and state. Point out other cities and states the student knows or is interested in. Student listens.
2. Teacher models the sentences. Student repeats after each sentence.

DRILL: Question and Answer Drill

Teacher asks questions to elicit vocabulary items.

Teacher	**Student**
What are Canada and the United States? They are big countries.	They are big countries.
How many states does the United States have? The United States has 50 states.	The United States has 50 states.

What is Canada?
How many cities does the United States have?
What country is a neighbor of the United States?
Where does Ann Baker live?
What city do you live in?
What state do you live in?

© New Readers Press. All rights reserved.

VOCABULARY: Idioms with *take* and *make*

I take a bus to work every morning.
I take a break at 10 o'clock.
I take English at school.
I take some medicine when I am sick.

I made an appointment with the doctor for a checkup.
I made a date with my friend to go to the movies.
I made a mistake and got on the wrong bus.
I made a mess when I dropped the food.

As you model the sentences, have the student listen to *take* and *made*.

Explain any of the idioms the student does not understand. For example, *take a break* means to stop working for a short time. *Make an appointment* is used for business, whereas *make a date* is used for social occasions.

DRILL: Making Sentences

Teacher gives the student a word or phrase which the student uses in a sentence with *take* or *make* (*made*).

Teacher	**Student**
a bus I take a bus to work every morning.	I take a bus to work every morning.
a mistake I made a mistake when I added the numbers.	I made a mistake when I added the numbers.

Teacher

a break	a date	English	a bus
an appointment	some medicine	a mess	

© New Readers Press. All rights reserved.

STRUCTURE FOCUS: *more ... than* with Nouns

She has three books
I have two books.
She has more books than I do.

David has three pencils.
Ed has one pencil.
David has more pencils than Ed does.

1. Teacher models each set of three sentences, asking the student to listen to *more ... than*.
   Student listens.
2. Teacher models each set of three sentences.
   Student repeats the sentence with *more ... than*.

Note: In these sentences *more* is used with nouns. It indicates a greater number and is used to compare two of anything.

DRILL: Combining Sentences

Teacher gives two sentences which the student combines into one using *more ... than*.

Teacher	Student
Ann has two dogs. Ed has one dog. Ann has more dogs than Ed does.	Ann has more dogs than Ed does.
She has four books. I have two books. She has more books than I do.	She has more books than I do.
We have three cats. They have two cats.	
She takes two buses to go to work. I take one bus to go to work.	
The Smiths have two cars. We have one car.	
The Smiths have three children. We have two children.	
Ann made three mistakes yesterday. Gail made two mistakes yesterday.	
I take two breaks at work every day. Ed takes one break at work every day.	

© New Readers Press. All rights reserved.

STRUCTURE FOCUS: Question Words + Infinitive

Please tell me	where	to put these books.
I don't know	what	to do.
Ann will teach you	how	to swim.
He's learning	how	to play hockey.

As you model each sentence, ask the student to listen to *where, what*, and *how*.

Note: The question words *when, where, who, what, how* may be followed by an infinitive.

DRILL: Completion Drill

Teacher gives the beginning of a sentence which the student completes using an infinitive.

Teacher	**Student**
Kay will teach me how Kay will teach me how to play cards.	Kay will teach me how to play cards.
I want to learn how I want to learn how to read.	I want to learn how to read.
Please tell me what	
I know where	
She wants to know how many plates	
Ann is going to teach me how	
They know when	

LISTENING COMPREHENSION

Pete runs the repair shop on Second Street. He fixes radios, TVs, and many other things. He makes money fixing things. But he really likes to teach hockey. He teaches teenagers to play hockey. They are having fun learning the game. They want to be the best hockey team in the valley.

1. Teacher reads the story twice at a normal pace.
   Student listens. Student asks about words he does not know.
2. Student tells the story in his own words. If the student cannot tell the story, teacher may begin the sentence and have the student complete it.

Note: If the student cannot remember the story, read it once or twice again.

© New Readers Press. All rights reserved.

ORAL EVALUATION

1. Using *LWE Illustrations 3*, p. 32, review the stages of life by identifying the illustrations. Student should know all the words.
2. Using *LWE Illustrations 3*, p. 33, review the words about Canada and the United States. Student should know all the words.
3. Review idioms *take* and *make* by doing the drill on Making Sentences. Student should know 6 of the idioms.
4. Review the use of *more ... than* with nouns by doing the drill on Combining Sentences.
5. Review the use of question words + infinitives by doing the Completion Drill.

II. Reading and Writing

BOOK 3: Lesson 10

Complete Lesson 10 in book 3, following the instructions given in *Laubach Way to Reading Teacher's Edition 3*. Adapt the wording of the suggested teacher's instructions to the student as necessary for your ESL student's comprehension.

ADDITIONAL WRITTEN PRACTICE

After completing Lesson 10 in book 3, have the student do the practices for Lesson 10 in workbook 3.

© New Readers Press. All rights reserved.

Lesson 11

OBJECTIVES

When a student completes this lesson, he should be able to:

1. Say and respond to a new dialog.
2. Say some words about date of birth.
3. Say some words about getting a driver's license.
4. Say some terms on an application.
5. Use simple *if* clauses.
6. Use *must* and *must not.*
7. Listen to a story and repeat it in his own words.

VISUAL AIDS

1. *LWE Illustrations 3*, pp. 34–35.
2. A driver's license.
3. An application for a driver's license, if it is possible to obtain one from your state.

I. Conversation Skills

DIALOG

A: Can I help you fill out your application?
B: Would you, please? I don't understand it.

A: What's the problem?
B: What does <u>M</u> or <u>F</u> mean?

A: <u>M</u> is for male, a man.
<u>F</u> is for female, a woman.
B: Oh, I see. That's easy.
What is a zip code?

A: It's the number the post office gives your state,
city, and street. It's part of your address.

© New Readers Press. All rights reserved.

VOCABULARY: Date of Birth

Ed is 20 years old. What is his age? It's 20.
He was born in ________ (year).
The date of his birth is January 1, 19____.
His birthday is on January 1.

Fill in the year of birth that will be accurate for a 20-year-old person.
Explain that it is not polite to ask a person what his age is.

DRILL: Answering Questions

Teacher asks questions to elicit the vocabulary.

Teacher	**Student**
How old is Ed? He is 20 years old.	He is 20 years old.
What is his age? He's 20.	He's 20.
When was Ed born? What is the date of Ed's birth? When is Ed's birthday? When is your birthday?	

VOCABULARY: Getting a Driver's License

Ed rides a bicycle to work.
He does not need a license to ride a bicycle.

David drives a car to work.
He needs a license to drive a car.
He needs license plates for his car.

You need to take a written test and
a driver's test to get a driver's license.
The person who gives the test is a tester.

Use *LWE Illustrations 3*, pp. 34–35. Also show an actual driver's license.

DRILL: Identification Drill

Teacher asks the question "What's this?" or "Who's this?" to elicit the vocabulary items. Point to the appropriate picture on pp. 34–35 of *LWE Illustrations 3*.

© New Readers Press. All rights reserved.

VOCABULARY: Terms on an Application

To get a driver's license, you need to fill out an application.

You have to write your name and address.
Your address is the street you live on, the city, the state,
and the post office zip code number.

You have to give your date of birth—the month, day, and year.
You have to give your sex—male or female.

Use an actual driver's license application or *LWE Illustrations 3*, p. 35.
Explain the words the student does not understand: *male* is man, *female* is woman.

DRILL: Answering Questions

Teacher asks questions which elicit the vocabulary items. Help the student with his personal information, but do not insist that he give his date of birth if he prefers not to.

Teacher	**Student**
What do you need to fill out to get a driver's license? You need to fill out an application.	You need to fill out an application.
What is a person's address? An address is a person's street, city, state, and zip code.	An address is a person's street, city, state, and zip code.

What does *date of birth* mean?
What does *male* mean?
What does *female* mean?
What is your address?
What is your zip code?
What is your birthday?
Are you male or female?

© New Readers Press. All rights reserved.

STRUCTURE FOCUS: *If* Clauses

<u>If</u> you pass the driver's test,
you will get a driver's license.

<u>If</u> Ray and Kay have enough money,
they will go away for three days.

As you model each sentence, ask the student to listen to *if.*

Note: These *if* clauses are true in the present or future time.
The simple present is used in the *if* clause; the future tense with *will* (or the present tense) is used in the main clause.

DRILL: Answering Questions

Teacher asks questions which elicit answers with *if* clauses.
Student replies may vary.

Teacher	**Student**
If you pass the driver's test, what will you get?	
If I pass the driver's test, I'll get a license.	If I pass the driver's test, I'll get a license.
What will Kay and Ray do if they have enough money?	
If Kay and Ray have enough money, they will go away.	If Kay and Ray have enough money, they will go away.

What will you buy if you have enough money?
What will you do if you have enough time?
Where will you go if you have some money?
What will you get if you pass the driver's test?

© New Readers Press. All rights reserved.

STRUCTURE FOCUS: The Use of *must* and *must not*

You must have a driver's license to drive a car.
You must stop for a red light.

You must not drive without a driver's license.
A person must not touch a hot stove.

As you model each sentence, ask the student to listen to *must* and *must not.*

Note: In the affirmative, *must* is used to indicate strong obligation.
In the negative, *must not* indicates that something is prohibited.

DRILL: Completion Drill

Teacher gives a phrase which the student uses in a sentence with *must* or *must not.*

Teacher	**Student**
stop for a red light You must stop for a red light.	You must stop for a red light.
drive without a driver's license You must not drive without a driver's license.	You must not drive without a driver's license.

go through a red light
touch a hot stove
stop for a red light
take a driver's test to get a driver's license
put your hand in the fire
drive without a license
write in library books

© New Readers Press. All rights reserved.

LISTING COMPREHENSION

In many states, when you are 16, you can get a permit to drive a car. With a permit, you can start driving, but a person with a driver's license must ride with you. When you think you can drive, you can take a driver's test. If you pass it, you can get a driver's license. Then you can drive alone.

1. Teacher reads the story twice at a normal pace.
   Student listens. Student asks about words he does not know.
2. Student tells the story in his own words. If the student cannot tell the story, teacher may begin the sentence and have the student complete it.

Note: If the student cannot remember the story, read it once or twice again.

ORAL EVALUATION

1. Review vocabulary on date of birth by doing the drill on Answering Questions. Student should be able to answer all of the questions.
2. Using *LWE Illustrations 3*, pp. 34–35, have the student say the words about getting a driver's license. Student should know all of them.
3. Using *LWE Illustrations 3*, p. 35, review terms on an application by doing the drill on Answering Questions. Student should be able to answer all the questions.
4. Review *if* clauses by doing the drill on Answering Questions.
5. Review *must* and *must not* by doing the Completion Drill.

II. Reading and Writing

BOOK 3: Lesson 11

Complete Lesson 11 in book 3, following the instructions given in *Laubach Way to Reading Teacher's Edition 3*. Adapt the wording of the suggested teacher's instructions to the student as needed for your ESL student's comprehension.

ADDITIONAL WRITTEN PRACTICE

After completing Lesson 11 in book 3, have the student do the practices for Lesson 11 in workbook 3.

© New Readers Press. All rights reserved.

Lesson 12

OBJECTIVES

When a student completes this lesson, he should be able to:

1. Say and respond to a new dialog.
2. Say words concerning length: *inch, foot, yard,* and *mile.*
3. Say words concerning feelings: *smile, laugh, frown,* and *cry.*
4. Say words about running in a race.
5. Say words about being retired.
6. Distinguish between *signing* and *printing* one's name.
7. Say the words *for sale, salesperson,* and *price.*
8. Use *has/have been* + verb-*ing*.
9. Use *while* clauses.
10. Review short answers to questions.
11. Listen to a story and repeat it in his own words.

VISUAL AIDS

A ruler or tape measure. (You will need to show an inch, a foot, and a yard.)

I. Conversation Skills

DIALOG

A: Are you going to watch Fran run in the race?
B: I didn't know she was going to run.

A: Yes, she's been running every day for three years.
She's a good runner.
B: I'd like to watch Fran run.
When is the race?

A: Next Saturday.
Let's go together.
B: OK.

© New Readers Press. All rights reserved.

VOCABULARY: Measures of Length

This is one <u>inch</u>.
There are 12 inches in a <u>foot</u>.
There are 3 feet in a <u>yard</u>.
There are 5,280 feet in one <u>mile</u>.

As you model the sentences, use a ruler or tape measure to show *inch, foot*, and *yard.*

Note: To give the student a better understanding of *mile*, you may also want to add a sentence (*It is a mile from* ____ *to* ____ .), using two places that he would recognize. Also, it would be helpful to know in advance the distance from your student's home to class for the drill that follows.

DRILL: Question and Answer Drill

Teacher asks "How long is this?" to elicit vocabulary items.
Point to a measure on the ruler or tape measure.

Teacher	Student
How long is this?	
It's one inch.	It's one inch.
How long is this?	
It's one foot.	It's one foot.

Teacher (pointing to the ruler)

6 inches
3 feet
1 foot
1 yard

Teacher

How tall are you?
How far is it from your house to class?

© New Readers Press. All rights reserved.

VOCABULARY: Verbs That Express Feelings

When Fran is happy, she smiles.
When something is funny, Fran laughs.
When Fran is not happy, she frowns.
When Fran is very sad, she cries.
When Fran is angry, she shouts.

Act out the new verbs to show their meaning.

DRILL: Question and Answer Drill

Teacher asks questions to elicit vocabulary items.

Teacher	Student
What does Fran do when she's happy? She smiles.	 She smiles.
What does Fran do when she is very sad? She cries.	 She cries.

What does Fran do when something is funny?
What does Fran do when she's happy?
What does Fran do when she's not happy?
What does Fran do when she's very sad?
What does Fran do when she's angry?

VOCABULARY: Running in a Race

Fran is going to run in a race with 14 other women.
Fran wants to run fast.
She wants to win the race.
The winner will finish first.
There's a tie when two people finish at the same time.

VOCABULARY: A Retired Couple

Retired people have time to do things that they like.

Some people are very busy.
They don't have time to do the things they like.

Mike and Fran are over 62 and are retired.
They don't have jobs any more.
They have time to do the things that they like.

© New Readers Press. All rights reserved.

VOCABULARY: *sign* and *print*

When you write a letter, you sign your name.
You print your name on an application.

Demonstrate signing and printing your name on the blackboard or a piece of paper.

DRILL: Identification Drill

1. Sign your name while saying, "I am signing my name."
   Then print your name while saying, "I am printing my name."
2. Perform each action again, asking "What am I doing?"

VOCABULARY: For Sale

The things in stores are for sale.
Food is for sale at a supermarket.
Furniture is for sale at a furniture store.
Medicine is for sale at a drugstore.

A salesperson in a store sells things.
The money you pay for a thing is the price.

DRILL: Answering Questions

Teacher asks questions to elicit the vocabulary. The prices in student replies may vary.

Teacher	Student
What is the price of a newspaper? The price is 50 cents.	The price is 50 cents.
What is for sale at a drugstore? Medicine is for sale at a drugstore.	Medicine is for sale at a drugstore.

What does a salesperson do?
What is the price of a coat?
What is for sale at a supermarket?
What is for sale at a department store?
What is the price of a newspaper?
What is for sale at a furniture store?
What is for sale at a drugstore?
What does a salesperson do?

© New Readers Press. All rights reserved.

STRUCTURE FOCUS: *have/has been* + Verb-*ing*

I'm tired. I	have	been	playing	hockey for three hours.
Fran	has	been	running	every day for three years.
Jason	has	been	going	to class for six months.
Carla and David	have	been	studying	for two hours.

As you model each sentence, ask the student to listen to *have been* and *has been.*

Note: The present perfect progressive tense is used to describe an action that began in the past and continues in the present.

DRILL: Answering Questions

Teacher asks a question which the student answers using *has been* or *have been* + verb-*ing*.

Teacher	**Student**
How long have you been studying? I have been studying for two hours.	I have been studying for two hours.
How long has Fran been running? She has been running for three years.	She has been running for three years.

How long have you been sitting here?
How long has Jason been going to class?
How long have Carla and David been studying?
How long have you been reading that book?
How long has Steve been working on the radio?
How long has Pete been teaching the boys to play hockey?

© New Readers Press. All rights reserved.

STRUCTURE FOCUS: *While* Clauses

While his wife runs, Mike makes breakfast.
While Carla studies, David watches Rosa.
While I was walking, it started to rain.
While Ray was making a salad, Kay cooked the meat.

As you model each sentence, ask the student to listen to *while*.

Note: *While* is used when two actions occur at the same time in the present or past.

DRILL: Answering Questions

Teacher asks questions which the student answers using *while*.
Student replies may vary.

Teacher	Student
What does Mike do while his wife runs?	
Mike makes breakfast while his wife runs.	Mike makes breakfast while his wife runs.
What was Carla doing while the teacher talked?	
Carla was listening while the teacher talked.	Carla was listening while the teacher talked.

What were you doing while Carla studied?
What were you doing while Ann telephoned Gail?
What was Kay doing while Ray was making a salad?
What does the teacher do while you read?
What does Mike do while his wife runs?
What do you do while the teacher talks?

© New Readers Press. All rights reserved.

STRUCTURE FOCUS: Review of Short Answers

Is Ann in class?	No, she isn't.
Are you ready?	Yes, I am.
Were they at the wedding party?	Yes, they were.
Was Tom angry?	No, he wasn't.
Do you have an English book?	Yes, I do.
Does this bus go to Main Street?	No, it doesn't.
Did Fran go running yesterday?	Yes, she did.
Have you read this book?	No, I haven't.
Has Fran been running for a year?	Yes, she has.
Can you play basketball?	No, I can't.
Will you help me?	Yes, I will.

1. Teacher models each question and answer, asking the student to listen to the short answer. Student listens.
2. Teacher models the question and answer. Student repeats the answer.

DRILL: Question and Answer Drill

Teacher asks a question which the student answers using a short answer.
Student replies may be affirmative or negative.

Teacher	Student
Are the children playing ball?	
No, they aren't.	No, they aren't.
Have you read this book?	
Yes, I have.	Yes, I have.

Can you play baseball?
Will you help me?
Was Fran crying?
Can we be ready by nine o'clock?
Does Fran sometimes get tired from running?
Is Mike White still working?
Are Fran and Mike retired?
Did you take a driver's test for your license?
Will you drive me home, please?
Can Jason fix the stairs?
Has Fran been running for a year?
Will they paint the kitchen gray?
Has Steve saved some money?
Have you tried to telephone Ann today?

© New Readers Press. All rights reserved.

LISTENING COMPREHENSION

Fran White likes to run. She has been running every day for three years. She gets up at five o'clock and runs. Sometimes, she runs in the park. Sometimes, she runs in the street. She is getting ready for a big race. It is a mile race for retired women. Fran wants to win the race.

1. Teacher reads the story twice at a normal pace.
   Student listens. Student asks about words he does not know.
2. Student tells the story in his own words. If the student cannot tell the story, teacher may begin the sentence and have the student complete it.

Note: If the student cannot remember the story, read it once or twice again.

ORAL EVALUATION

1. Review measures of length by doing the Question and Answer Drill. Student should be able to answer 5 items.
2. Review terms for feelings by doing the Question and Answer Drill. Student should be able to answer all of the items.
3. Review the terms for running in a race. Ask questions that elicit the vocabulary items. Student should know 4 of them.
4. Review the vocabulary about the retired couple, asking questions that elicit the items. Student should know the meaning of *retired.*
5. Review *signing* and *printing* one's name. Student should be able to distinguish these terms and to recognize that both are writing.
6. Review the present perfect progressive tense by doing the drill on Answering Questions.
7. Review *while* clauses by doing the drill on Answering Questions.

II. Reading and Writing

BOOK 3: Lesson 12

Complete Lesson 12 in book 3, following the instructions given in *Laubach Way to Reading Teacher's Edition 3*. Adapt the wording of the suggested teacher's instructions to the student as needed for your ESL student's comprehension.

ADDITIONAL WRITTEN PRACTICE

After completing Lesson 12 in book 3, have the student do the practices for Lesson 12 in workbook 3.

© New Readers Press. All rights reserved.

Lesson 13

OBJECTIVES

When a student completes this lesson, he should be able to:

1. Say and respond to a new dialog.
2. Say some words related to church services.
3. Say some expressions of sympathy.
4. Say some words related to flying.
5. Say some words that name periods of time.
6. Use *It* + *be* + infinitive, as in *It's time to eat.*
7. Use *It takes* + time expressions + infinitive, as in *It takes me an hour to get to work.*
8. Make tag questions with *be* (*is, are, was, were*), as in *It's a nice day, isn't it*?
9. Give the expected answers to tag questions.
10. Make questions with *why*.
11. Listen to a story and repeat it in his own words.

VISUAL AIDS

1. *LWE Illustrations 3*, pp. 36–39.
2. A watch, preferably with a second hand.
3. A calendar for a full year.

I. Conversation Skills

DIALOG

A: The weather is terrible.
I hate rain.
B: Me, too.
I haven't been able to go fishing all week.

A: You must like to fish.
B: Yes, it's my favorite way to spend my free time.

A: Where do you go fishing?
B: At Snake River.

A: That's a good place to fish, isn't it?
B: Yes, it is.

© New Readers Press. All rights reserved.

VOCABULARY: Church Services

Mike and Fran go to church on Sunday.
They pray together.
They listen to the minister in church.
The minister leads the services in church.

When Fran's brother died, there was a funeral.
There were services in church for Fran's dead brother.
After the services, they went to the cemetery.
Friends put flowers on the grave.

Use *LWE Illustrations 3*, pp. 36–37.

DRILL: Question and Answer Drill

Teacher asks questions to elicit vocabulary items.

Teacher	**Student**
Where do Mike and Fran go on Sunday?	
They go to church on Sunday.	They go to church on Sunday.
Who do Mike and Fran listen to in church?	
They listen to the minister.	They listen to the minister.

What does the minister do in church?
What was there in church when Fran's brother died?
Who do Mike and Fran listen to in church?
Who were the services in church for?
Where did they go after the services?
What did friends put on the grave?
What do people do in church?

© New Readers Press. All rights reserved.

VOCABULARY: Expressions of Sympathy

I lost all my money.	That's a shame.
She broke her leg.	What a pity.
The child was crying.	Her mother picked her up and said, "There, there."

1. Teacher models each pair of sentences. Student listens.

2. Teacher models each pair of sentences.
   Student repeats the expression of sympathy.

DRILL: Rejoinder Drill

Teacher makes a statement, to which the student replies with an expression of sympathy.

Teacher	**Student**
When a child is crying, what do you say? There, there.	There, there.
When Ed is sick, what do you say? What a pity.	What a pity.
When Kay loses her sweater, what do you say?	
When a child is crying, what do you say?	
When Steve loses his money, what do you say?	
When Ed is sick, what do you say?	

© New Readers Press. All rights reserved.

VOCABULARY: Flying

Mike and Fran are going to fly to King City.
They are going to fly on a big airplane high in the sky.
They will get their tickets at the air line.*

Their flight to King City leaves at 9:30 a.m.
It is in the morning.

There is another flight to King City at 9:30 p.m.
It is at night.

The pilot will fly the plane.
The flight attendant will give them a cup of coffee.

*Tell students that they will often see *airline* written as a compound word.

Use *LWE Illustrations 3*, pp. 38–39.

DRILL: Question and Answer Drill

Teacher asks questions to elicit vocabulary items.

Teacher	**Student**
How are Mike and Fran going to King City?	
They are going to fly to King City.	They are going to fly to King City.
What are they going to fly on?	
They are going to fly on a big airplane.	They are going to fly on a big airplane.

Where will they get their tickets?
Who flies the plane?
Who gives Mike and Fran coffee?
When does their flight to King City leave?
How are Mike and Fran going to King City?
What are they going to fly on?

© New Readers Press. All rights reserved.

VOCABULARY: Time

There are 60 seconds in one minute.
There are 60 minutes in one hour.
There are 24 hours in one day.
There are 30 or 31 days in one month.
There are 12 months in one year.

Use a clock or watch and a calendar for a full year to explain the words.

DRILL: Answering Questions

Teacher asks questions which elicit the vocabulary being taught.

Teacher	**Student**
How many seconds are there in a minute? There are 60 seconds in a minute.	There are 60 seconds in a minute.
How many minutes are there in an hour? There are 60 minutes in an hour.	There are 60 minutes in an hour.
How many hours are there in a day? How many days are there in a month? How many months are there in a year? How many minutes are there in an hour? How many seconds are there in a minute?	

STRUCTURE FOCUS: *It's* + *time* + (*for*) + Infinitive

It's time	to eat.	
It's time	to go to bed.	
It's time	for Fran	to run.
It's time	for me	to go to work.

As you model each sentence, ask the student to listen to *It's time to.*

DRILL: Making Sentences

Teacher has the student make sentences using *It's time* and *It's time to.*

Teacher	**Student**
It's time It's time to study.	It's time to study.
It's time for Fran It's time for Fran to run.	It's time for Fran to run.
It's time for Mike It's time for Mike and Fran It's time for the teacher It's time for you It's time for my son (daughter) It's time for me It's time	

© New Readers Press. All rights reserved.

STRUCTURE FOCUS: *It* + *takes* + Time Expressions + Infinitive

It takes me 30 minutes	to get to work.
It takes me an hour	to bake a cake.

As you model each sentence, ask the student to listen to *It takes*.

DRILL: Answering Questions

Teacher asks a question which the student answers using *It takes*.
Student replies may vary.

Teacher	Student
How long does it take you to get to work? It takes me 30 minutes.	It takes me 30 minutes.
How long does it take you to bake a cake? It takes me an hour.	It takes me an hour.

How long does it take you to get to work?
How long does it take you to get to class?
How long does it take you to get to the post office?
How long does it take you to get to your friend's house?
How long does it take you to make breakfast?
How long does it take you to make dinner?
How long does it take you to do dishes?
How long does it take you to do your homework?

© New Readers Press. All rights reserved.

STRUCTURE FOCUS: Tag Questions with *be*

It's a nice day,	isn't it?
She was a waitress,	wasn't she?
You are Italian,	aren't you?
There are tomatoes in the salad,	aren't there?
Carla wasn't going camping,	was she?
You aren't married,	are you?
Gail and Jason weren't here,	were they?
We aren't leaving now,	are we?

As you model each sentence, ask the student to listen to *isn't it, wasn't she*, and so on.

Note: When the first (statement) part of the sentence is affirmative, the tag question is negative.

When the first part of the sentence is negative, the tag question is affirmative.

Both verbs are in the same tense.
A pronoun is always used in the tag question.

DRILL: Making Questions

Teacher makes a statement to which the student adds a tag question.

Teacher	**Student**
It's a nice day. It's a nice day, isn't it?	It's a nice day, isn't it?
Ann wasn't sick. Ann wasn't sick, was she?	Ann wasn't sick, was she?

Carla wasn't going camping.
You are Italian.
Ray and Kay are married.
It wasn't a nice day yesterday.
We're leaving now.
Gail and Jason weren't here yesterday.
Ann wasn't sick.
There are tomatoes in the salad.
He's a minister.
There isn't any sugar in the tea.

© New Readers Press. All rights reserved.

STRUCTURE FOCUS: Expected Answers to Tag Questions

It's a nice day, isn't it?	Yes, it is.
You are married, aren't you?	Yes, I am.
Pete wasn't here yesterday, was he?	No, he wasn't.
Ann wasn't late, was she?	No, she wasn't.

1. Teacher models each question and answer, asking the student to listen to the answer.

2. Teacher models the question and answer. Student repeats each answer.

Note: Generally in tag questions, when confirmation or agreement is being solicited, the short reply agrees with the statement. If it is an affirmative statement, agreement is expressed with *Yes*. If it is a negative statement, agreement is expressed with *No*.

Some students may not be accustomed to expressing agreement with *No* in similar constructions in their own language and may think the answer should be *Yes, he wasn't.*

DRILL: Answering Questions

Teacher asks a tag question, which the student answers using short answers.

Teacher	**Student**
It's a nice day, isn't it? Yes, it is.	Yes, it is.
Pete wasn't here yesterday, was he? No, he wasn't.	No, he wasn't.

Carla isn't going camping, is she?
You are Italian, aren't you?
Ray and Kay are married, aren't they?
It was a nice day yesterday, wasn't it?
There are tomatoes in the salad, aren't there?
We're leaving now, aren't we?
Gail and Jason weren't here yesterday, were they?
Ann wasn't sick, was she?
There isn't any sugar in the tea, is there?
He's a minister, isn't he?

© New Readers Press. All rights reserved.

STRUCTURE FOCUS: Questions with *why*

Fran runs five miles every day.
Why does Fran run five miles every day?

Lee hit the tree.
Why did Lee hit the tree?

Fran has been crying.
Why has Fran been crying?

1. Teacher models each pair of sentences, asking the student to listen to *why*.
2. Teacher models each pair of sentences. Student repeats the question with *why*.

DRILL: Making Questions

Teacher gives a statement which the student changes into a question with *why*.

Teacher	**Student**
Fran has been crying. Why has Fran been crying?	Why has Fran been crying?
Steve saves some of his money. Why does Steve save some of his money?	Why does Steve save some of his money?
Fran runs five miles every day.	
Mike White is at home.	
Mrs. Green was angry at Lee.	
Lee hit the tree.	
Fran was crying.	
They eat a lot of beans.	
Jill has two part-time jobs.	
You are studying English.	

LISTENING COMPREHENSION

Tom Roberts died in his sleep one night. His family and his friends were very sad to hear about Tom. They loved him, and they missed him. They came to see Tom's wife Ellen to try to help her. They talked about the good times they had with Ellen and Tom. They cried together.

Tom's family and friends went to the church services for Tom. The minister said some nice things about Tom. It was a sad day for everyone.

1. Teacher reads the story twice at a normal pace.
   Student listens. Student asks about words he does not know.
2. Student tells the story in his own words. If the student cannot tell the story, teacher may begin the sentence and have the student complete it.

Note: If the student cannot remember the story, read it once or twice again.

© New Readers Press. All rights reserved.

ORAL EVALUATION

1. Using *LWE Illustrations 3*, pp. 36–37, review the vocabulary on church services by doing the Question and Answer Drill. Student should know 7 items.
2. Practice expressions of sympathy by doing the Rejoinder Drill. Student should know all of the items.
3. Using *LWE Illustrations 3*, pp. 38–39, practice words about flying by doing the Question and Answer Drill. Student should know 8 of the items.
4. Review words about time by doing the drill on Answering Questions. Student should know all of the items.
5. Review *It's* + *time* + (*for*) + infinitive by doing the drill on Making Sentences.
6. Review *It* + *takes* + time expressions + infinitive by doing the drill on Answering Questions.
7. Review the use of tag questions with *be* by doing the drill on Making Questions.
8. Review the expected answers to tag questions by doing the drill on Answering Questions.
9. Review questions with *why* by doing the drill on Making Questions.

II. Reading and Writing

BOOK 3: Lesson 13

Complete Lesson 13 in book 3, following the instructions given in *Laubach Way to Reading Teacher's Edition 3*. Adapt the wording of the suggested teacher's instructions to the student as needed for your ESL student's comprehension.

ADDITIONAL WRITTEN PRACTICE

After completing Lesson 13 in book 3, have the student do the practices for Lesson 13 in workbook 3.

© New Readers Press. All rights reserved.

Lesson 14

OBJECTIVES

When a student completes this lesson, he should be able to:

1. Say and respond to a new dialog.
2. Use *get* and some adjectives.
3. Use words having to do with an air line timetable.
4. Use the phrase *in sight.*
5. Use some adjectives: *worry, afraid, angry, interested, tired, right, wrong.*
6. Use adjectives + prepositions + nouns, as in *She is angry at Lee.*
7. Use *should* in affirmative and negative statements, questions, and short answers.
8. Use tag questions with *do, does, did.*
9. Use tag questions with other verbs.
10. Use *because* in answers to questions with *why.*
11. Use *as ... as* with adjectives and adverbs, as in *Fran runs as fast as Kim does.*
12. Listen to a story and repeat it in his own words.

VISUAL AIDS

The air line timetable in book 3, p. 79.

I. Conversation Skills

DIALOG

A: Excuse me.
Can you tell me where the plane to Dallas is?
B: It departs from Gate 5.

A: Pardon me.
B: The plane for Dallas leaves from Gate 5.

A: Where is Gate 5?
B: Turn left, and walk past Gates 1, 2, and 3.

A: Thank you.
B: You're welcome.

© New Readers Press. All rights reserved.

VOCABULARY: *get* + Adjectives

It	is getting	cold.
My son	is getting	tall.
They	got	ready to paint.
My hair	is getting	gray.

Note: The verb *get*, followed by certain adjectives, means *become*.

DRILL: Making Sentences

Teacher names an adjective, and the student uses it in a sentence with *get*.

Teacher	**Student**
old I am getting old.	I am getting old.
gray My hair is getting gray.	My hair is getting gray.
cold	
light	
well	
dark	
fast	

VOCABULARY: Air Line Timetable

Air lines have a timetable of flights to and from many cities.
The timetable tells when the air line departs and when it arrives.
The timetable tells which gate the airplane will be at.

Use book 3, p. 79, to show an air line timetable.

VOCABULARY: The Use of *in sight*

I can see the church from here.
It's in sight.

Lee can see the lights of his city from the airplane.
They are still in sight.

The river is very far from here.
It's not in sight.

© New Readers Press. All rights reserved.

VOCABULARY: Adjectives about Feelings

Pete is worried. His mother is very sick.
Mrs. Green is angry. It's half past three, and Lee isn't home.
Ed was afraid. Lee was driving the car very fast.
Carla was right. She said I needed a license to drive a car.
Ed was wrong. He said I didn't need a license to drive a car.
I am tired. I worked ten hours today.
I am interested. This book is very good.

STRUCTURE FOCUS: Adjectives + Prepositions + Nouns

Pete is	worried about	his mother.
Mrs. Green is	angry at	Lee.
Ed is	afraid of	the dog.
Carla was	right about	the time.
Ed was	wrong about	the price.
I am	tired of	television.
I am	interested in	good books.

As you model each sentence, ask the student to listen to *worry about, angry at*, and so on.

DRILL: Answering Questions

Teacher asks questions which elicit an adjective + preposition in the answer.

Teacher	**Student**
What is Pete worried about? He's worried about his mother.	He's worried about his mother.
Who is Mrs. Green angry at? She's angry at Lee.	She's angry at Lee.

What is Ed afraid of?
What was Carla right about?
What was Ed wrong about?
What is Pete worried about?
Who is Mrs. Green angry at?
What are you tired of?
What are you interested in?

© New Readers Press. All rights reserved.

STRUCTURE FOCUS: Adjectives + Prepositions + Verb-*ing*

Lee Chan is	worried about	leaving his country.
Ed is	afraid of	swimming in cold water.
I am	tired of	watching TV.
I am	interested in	learning about China.

As you model each sentence, ask the student to listen to the *-ing: leaving, swimming, watching*, and *learning*.

DRILL: Making Questions

Teacher asks questions which elicit adjectives + prepositions + verb-*ing*.

Teacher	**Student**
What is Lee Chan worried about? He's worried about leaving China.	He's worried about leaving China.
What is Ed afraid of? He's afraid of swimming in cold water.	He's afraid of swimming in cold water.
What is Lee Chan worried about? What is Ed afraid of? What is Fran interested in? What are you tired of? What are you interested in?	

© New Readers Press. All rights reserved.

STRUCTURE FOCUS: The Use of *should*

You should stop smoking.
They should listen to their parents.

You shouldn't smoke.
Ann shouldn't spend a lot of money.

Should I buy the red dress?	No, you shouldn't.
Should we leave now?	Yes, we should.

As you model each statement or question-and-answer, ask the student to listen to *should*—or *shouldn't*. Explain what *smoking* means.

Note: *Should* is used to express advisability; however, we do not very often do the things we say we should.

DRILL: Making Questions

Teacher gives a statement which the student must change into the question form and then answer.

Teacher	**Student**
You should stop smoking.	
Should I stop smoking?	Should I stop smoking?
Yes, I should.	Yes, I should.
Ann should buy the red dress.	
Should Ann buy the red dress?	Should Ann buy the red dress?
No, she shouldn't.	No, she shouldn't.

We should leave now.
We should pay our bills.
Lee should pay for the tree.
Pete should fix the radio.
Ann should leave early.
Carla should study her lesson.
Ed should get a driver's license.
Mike should make breakfast.
Ann should spend a lot of money.

© New Readers Press. All rights reserved.

STRUCTURE FOCUS: Tag Questions with *do, does, did*

The Masons have to pay a lot of bills, don't they?
You don't have to have license plates for a bicycle, do you?
Gail and Jason rented an apartment, didn't they?
Lee didn't see the tree, did he?

As you model each sentence, ask the student to listen to the tag question.

DRILL: Making Questions

Teacher gives a statement, to which the student adds a tag question.

Teacher	**Student**
Lee has to pay for the tree.	
Lee has to pay for the tree, doesn't he?	Lee has to pay for the tree, doesn't he?
Lee didn't see the tree.	
Lee didn't see the tree, did he?	Lee didn't see the tree, did he?

Fran cried about her brother.
Tom Roberts died in his sleep.
The Masons have to pay a lot of bills.
Ann goes to class at night.
You live near the school.
You have to take tests to get a driver's license.

© New Readers Press. All rights reserved.

STRUCTURE FOCUS: Tag Questions with Other Verbs

Jason and Gail have never painted a kitchen,	have they?
Fran has been running a long time,	hasn't she?
You can fix the radio,	can't you?
Lee can't play hockey,	can he?
They will play hockey in Canada,	won't they?
Lee will not be late again,	will he?
Ann should stop smoking,	shouldn't she?
Tom shouldn't spend so much money,	should he?

As you model each sentence, ask the student to listen to the tag question.

DRILL: Making Questions

Teacher gives a statement, to which the student adds a tag question.

Teacher	**Student**
You can fix the radio. You can fix the radio, can't you?	You can fix the radio, can't you?
Fran hasn't been playing soccer. Fran hasn't been playing soccer, has she?	Fran hasn't been playing soccer, has she?

Tom shouldn't spend so much money.
Lee will not be late again.
Gail and Jason have never painted a kitchen.
You can fix the radio.
Ann should stop smoking.
Retired people can get things for cheaper prices.
They will play hockey in Canada.
Fran has been running a long time.

© New Readers Press. All rights reserved.

STRUCTURE FOCUS: *Because* Clauses

Why is Lee Chan sad?
Because he is leaving his family.

Why was Fran crying?
Because her brother died in his sleep.

Why does Fran run five miles every day?
Because she wants to win the race.

1. Teacher models each question and answer, asking the student to listen to *because*. Student listens.

2. Teacher models each question and answer. Student repeats the answer.

DRILL: Question and Answer Drill

Teacher asks a question, which the student answers using *because*.
Student replies may vary.

Teacher	**Student**
Why is Lee Chan sad? Because he is leaving his family.	Because he is leaving his family.
Why does Gail have two part-time jobs? Because she needs the money.	Because she needs the money.
Why was Fran crying?	
Why does Fran run five miles every day?	
Why does Mike White stay at home?	
Why was Mrs. Green angry at Lee?	
Why did Lee hit the tree?	
Why are you studying English?	

© New Readers Press. All rights reserved.

STRUCTURE FOCUS: *as* + Adjective/Adverb + *as*

This pencil is	as long as	that one.
This book is	as big as	that one.
Her hair is	as dark as	Gail's.
Mrs. Green is	as angry as	I am.
Fran runs	as fast as	Kim does.

As you model each sentence, ask the student to listen to *as ... as*.

Note: *As ... as* is used with adjectives and adverbs to discuss two people or things that are alike. Show the students two objects that are the same length or size, such as two pencils or books.

DRILL: Combining Sentences

Teacher gives two sentences, which the student combines using *as ... as*.

Teacher	**Student**
Pete is sad. Lee is sad. Pete is as sad as Lee.	Pete is as sad as Lee.
This book is big. That book is big. This book is as big as that one.	This book is as big as that one.
Jane's hair is dark. Gail's hair is dark.	
Mrs. Green is angry. I am angry.	
Fran is happy. Mike is happy.	
Fran runs fast. Kim runs fast.	
Chan speaks slowly. I speak slowly.	
Pete is sad. Lee is sad.	
This book is small. That book is small.	

© New Readers Press. All rights reserved.

LISTENING COMPREHENSION

Lee Chan is from China. He left China to study in the United States. He left his wife and child in China. He will not see them for four years. It makes Lee sad to think of his family.

Lee is going to study hard. He wants to have a better job when he goes back to China. He wants to take care of his family better. And he wants to help China.

---

1. Teacher reads the story twice at a normal pace.
   Student listens. Student asks about words he does not know.

2. Student tells the story in his own words. If the student cannot tell the story, teacher may begin the sentence and have the student complete it.

Note: If the student cannot remember the story, read it once or twice again.

ORAL EVALUATION

1. Review the use of *get* + adjectives. Student should know all items.
2. Using the timetable in book 3, p. 79, have the student identify words about timetables. Student should know all items.
3. Review the adjectives. Student should know all of them.
4. Review adjectives + prepositions + nouns by doing the drill on Making Questions.
5. Review adjectives + prepositions + verb-*ing* by doing the drill on Making Questions.
6. Review *should* by doing the drill on Making Questions.
7. Review tag questions with *do*, *does*, and *did* by doing the drill on Making Questions.
8. Review tag questions with other verbs by doing the drill on Making Questions.
9. Review *because* clauses by doing the Question and Answer Drill.
10. Review *as* + adjective/adverb + *as* by doing the drill on Combining Sentences.

II. Reading and Writing

BOOK 3: Lesson 14

Complete Lesson 14 in book 3, following the instructions given in *Laubach Way to Reading Teacher's Edition 3*. Adapt the wording of the suggested teacher's instructions to the student as needed for your ESL student's comprehension.

ADDITIONAL WRITTEN PRACTICE

After completing Lesson 14 in book 3, have the student do the practices for Lesson 14 in workbook 3.

© New Readers Press. All rights reserved.

Lesson 15

OBJECTIVES

When a student completes this lesson, he should be able to:

1. Say and respond to a new dialog.
2. Use the word *almost*.
3. Use words about driving a car.
4. Use irregular noun plurals: *knives, wives, leaves, loaves, shelves,* and *men, women, children, feet, teeth.*
5. Use the comparative of adjectives.
6. Use the comparative of *good, bad, little*, and *far*.
7. Use *something/anything* + adjective + infinitive, as in *I want something hot to drink.*
8. Use *think* and *say* + noun clauses, as in *I think that he is a fine person.*
9. Listen to a story and repeat it in his own words.

VISUAL AIDS

1. An ID card or a driver's license or both.
2. Two small markers that can be used to represent cars, or two toy cars.

I. Conversation Skills

DIALOG

A: Would you cash this check for me, please?
B: Do you have an account at this bank?

A: Yes, I have a savings account.
B: Do you have any ID?

A: What?
B: Do you have any identification?

A: I have a driver's license.
And I have an ID card from work.
It has my picture on it.
B: Oh, good. Those are fine.

© New Readers Press. All rights reserved.

VOCABULARY: The Use of *almost*

It's 8:45. It's almost 9 o'clock.
My birthday is next month. I'm going to be 35. I'm almost 35.
I will be ready in five minutes. I'm almost ready.

1. Teacher models each group of 2–3 sentences, asking the student to listen to *almost.* Student listens.

2. Teacher models each group of sentences. Student repeats each sentence.

DRILL: Expansion Drill

Teacher makes a statement to which the student adds the word *almost.*

Teacher	Student
I am 35.	
I am almost 35.	I am almost 35.
It is 9 o'clock.	
It is almost 9 o'clock.	It is almost 9 o'clock.
It's 10 o'clock.	
I am 35.	
I am ready.	
He is finished.	
It's October.	
It's time to stop work.	

VOCABULARY: Driving a Car

Jill is learning how to drive a car.
She is learning how to go forward.
She is learning how to back up.
She is learning to make left and right turns.
She is learning to pass other cars.
She is learning to park the car.

Demonstrate the meaning of the new words using small markers to represent cars or toy cars.

© New Readers Press. All rights reserved.

STRUCTURE FOCUS: Irregular Noun Plurals

knife	knives	I have a knife. I have two knives.
wife	wives	I have a wife. My two sons have wives.
leaf	leaves	I have a leaf. I have two leaves.
loaf	loaves	I have a loaf of bread. I have two loaves of bread.
shelf	shelves	I have a shelf. I have two shelves.

1. Teacher models each pair of words.
   Explain the meaning of any words the student does not know.

2. Teacher models each pair of sentences.
   Student repeats after each sentence.

DRILL: Transformation Drill

Teacher gives a sentence in the singular, which the student changes into the plural, using the number *two*.

Teacher	**Student**
I have a knife. I have two knives.	I have two knives.
There is a wife. There are two wives.	There are two wives.

There is a leaf on the tree.
There is a loaf of bread in the kitchen.
There is a shelf in the room.
There is a wife.
I have a knife.

© New Readers Press. All rights reserved.

STRUCTURE FOCUS: More Irregular Noun Plurals

child	children	I have a child. I have two children.
man	men	A man is in the room. Two men are in the room.
woman	women	A woman is behind the table. Two women are behind the table.
foot	feet	My foot hurts. My feet hurt.
tooth	teeth	My tooth aches. My teeth ache.

1. Teacher models each pair of words.
   Explain the meaning of any words the student does not know.

2. Teacher models each pair of sentences.
   Student repeats after each sentence.

DRILL: Transformation Drill

Teacher gives a sentence in the singular which the student changes into the plural.

Teacher	**Student**
The child is happy. The children are happy.	 The children are happy.
My foot hurts. My feet hurt.	 My feet hurt.
My tooth aches. The man is in the room. The woman is behind the table. The child is happy. My foot hurts.	

© New Readers Press. All rights reserved.

STRUCTURE FOCUS: The Comparative of Adjectives

Mary is 20. Jane is 18.
Jane is younger than Mary.

Ed is 40. Tom is 30.
Ed is older than Tom.

Milk is 98¢. Cheese is $1.15.
Milk is cheaper than cheese.

Mike is sad. Fran is very sad.
Fran is sadder than Mike.

---

1. Teacher models each group of sentences, asking the student to listen to *younger than, older than*, and so on. Student listens.

2. Teacher models each group of sentences.
   Student repeats the sentence with *-er than*.

DRILL: Making Sentences

Teacher gives two sentences–and an adjective if the sentences themselves do not have one. Student uses them to make a statement with the comparative form of an adjective.

Teacher	**Student**
Kay is angry. Mary is very angry. Mary is angrier than Kay.	Mary is angrier than Kay.
Mary is 22. Jane is 18. (young) Jane is younger than Mary.	Jane is younger than Mary.
Milk is 98¢. Cheese is $1.15. (cheap)	
My house has 2 bedrooms. Your house has 3 bedrooms. (large)	
John is 15. Sam is 18. (old)	
Carla's hair is dark. Steve's hair is very dark.	
My dog is big. My cat is not big.	
Mike is sad. Fran is very sad.	

© New Readers Press. All rights reserved.

STRUCTURE FOCUS: Comparative of *good, bad, little, far*

This dark bread is good.
This dark bread is better than this white bread.

This movie is bad.
This movie is worse than that one.

I have little money.
I have less money than Ken.

My house is far.
My house is farther than your house.

---

1. Teacher models each pair of sentences, asking the student to listen to *better, worse, less,* and *farther*. Student listens.

2. Teacher models each pair of sentences.
   Student repeats the sentence containing the comparative.

DRILL: Combining Sentences

Teacher gives two sentences, which the student combines using a comparative.

Teacher	**Student**
I have little money. Ken has very little money. Ken has less money than I do.	Ken has less money than I do.
This movie is bad. That movie was very bad. That movie was worse than this one.	That movie was worse than this one.
This white bread is good. That dark bread is very good.	
This coffee is bad. That coffee is very bad.	
My house is far. Your house is very far.	
This book is bad. That book is very bad.	
I drink little milk. My husband drinks very little milk.	
The bank is far. The post office is very far.	

© New Readers Press. All rights reserved.

STRUCTURE FOCUS: *something/anything* + Adjective + Infinitive

Ellen has	something	sad	to tell you.
I want	something	hot	to drink.
I don't have	anything	clean	to wear.
I can't find	anything	interesting	to read.

As you model each sentence, ask the student to listen to *something sad to tell you*, and so on.

DRILL: Making Questions

Teacher gives the beginning of a question, such as *Do you have something nice*. Student completes the question with an infinitive or infinitive phrase.

Teacher	**Student**
Do you want something hot	
Do you want something hot to drink?	Do you want something hot to drink?
Do you have something good	
Do you have something good to tell me?	Do you have something good to tell me?
Do you have something nice	
Does Ellen have something sad	
Do you have something green	
Do you want something cold	
Can you find anything clean	
Can you find anything interesting	

© New Readers Press. All rights reserved.

STRUCTURE FOCUS: *think* or *say* + Noun Clauses

I think that he is a fine person.
Lee thinks that prices are high in the United States.
Ellen said that Tom died in his sleep.
They said that Tom was a fine man.

As you model each sentence, ask the student to listen to *think that* or *said that.*

Note: These noun clauses are objects of the verb *think* or *say*. The word *that* has no meaning in itself and is often omitted.

DRILL: Making Sentences

Teacher makes a statement and gives a subject. The student must make a statement with *think* or *say* and a noun clause.

Teacher	Student
Mike is a fine man. (I) I think that Mike is a fine man.	I think that Mike is a fine man.
Tom died in his sleep. (Ellen) Ellen said that Tom died in his sleep.	Ellen said that Tom died in his sleep.
Prices in the United States are high. (Lee)	
Jill did not stop at a stop sign. (The tester)	
I am ready for the mile race. (I)	
It was OK for Fran to run. (The doctor)	
Mike is a fine man. (You)	
Tom died in his sleep. (Ellen)	

© New Readers Press. All rights reserved.

LISTENING COMPREHENSION

Ellen and Tom Roberts had a happy life together. They were married for 29 years. And then Tom died in his sleep one night. Ellen was very sad, and she cried and cried. Her family helped her at first. But then they had to leave, and she was alone. Ellen had to learn to live by herself. She had to find a job. She had to start a new life for herself.

---

1. Teacher reads the story twice at a normal pace.
   Student listens. Student asks about words he does not know.

2. Student tells the story in his own words. If the student cannot tell the story, teacher may begin the sentence and have the student complete it.

Note: If the student cannot remember the story, read it once or twice again.

ORAL EVALUATION

1. Review the use of *almost* by doing the Expansion Drill.
2. By demonstrating the verbs, review the vocabulary on driving a car.
   Student should know 4 of the items.
3. Review the irregular noun plurals by doing both Transformation Drills.
   Student should know 8 of the items.
4. Review the comparative of *good, bad, little,* and *far*, by doing the drill on Combining Sentences.
5. Review *something/anything* + adjective + infinitive by doing the drill on Making Questions.
6. Review *think* and *say* + noun clauses by doing the drill on Making Sentences.

II. Reading and Writing

BOOK 3: Lesson 15

Complete Lesson 15 in book 3, following the instructions given in *Laubach Way to Reading Teacher's Edition 3*. Adapt the wording of the suggested teacher's instructions to the student as needed for your ESL student's comprehension.

ADDITIONAL WRITTEN PRACTICE

After completing Lesson 15 in book 3, have the student do the practices for Lesson 15 in workbook 3.

© New Readers Press. All rights reserved.

Lesson 16

OBJECTIVES

When a student completes this lesson, he should be able to:

1. Say and respond to a new dialog.
2. Say the story words *gold* and *silver.*
3. Use the expressions *Oh; Oh, no*; and *Oh, well.*
4. Say the names of some city workers.
5. Use the word *both.*
6. Say the past participle of irregular verbs: *break* (*broken*), *choose* (*chosen*), *drive* (*driven*), *freeze* (*frozen*), *ride* (*ridden*), and *steal* (*stolen*).
7. Use the passive voice.
8. Use the passive with *get*, as in *I got tired.*
9. Use *can* and *could.*
10. Use *if* clauses, as in *I can't tell if he is right.*
11. Use clauses with *so*, as in *I am tired, so I am going to bed.*
12. Listen to a story and repeat it in his own words.

VISUAL AIDS

1. *LWE Illustrations 3*, pp. 40–41.
2. A gold ring.
3. A silver ring.

I. Conversation Skills

DIALOG

A: I need a new sofa, but I don't have much money.
B: Why don't you look at the ads in the paper?

A: What's in the ads?
B: Sometimes they have sofas that people want to sell.
They cost less than new ones.

A: That's what I need—a sofa that costs less.
I don't have the money for a new sofa.
B: I bet you'll find a cheap one in the ads.

A: Thanks for the advice.

VOCABULARY: Gold and Silver

Gold rings are expensive.
Usually, silver rings cost less than gold rings.

Use a gold ring and a silver ring to show the meaning of the new words.

© New Readers Press. All rights reserved.

VOCABULARY: Expressions with *Oh*

Oh, good! I have a letter from my sister.
Oh, my head! It really hurts.
Oh, no! I have a parking ticket.
Joe isn't home. Oh, well. I'll call him later.
Fran didn't win the race. Oh, well, she can try again.

Act out the meaning of the expressions. Say the words with feeling.

DRILL: Rejoinder Drill

Teacher makes a statement which elicits an expression with *Oh* from the student.

Teacher	Student
I have a letter from my sister. Oh, good.	Oh, good.
Our team lost the game. Oh, no.	Oh, no.
I didn't see Joe. Oh, well. You can try again tomorrow.	Oh, well. You can try again tomorrow.

I hurt my leg.
I have a parking ticket.
I don't have any money.
Fran didn't win the race.
Joe isn't home.
My baby is feeling better.
My TV isn't working.

VOCABULARY: Public Employees

Police officers work for the police department.
They carry guns.

Firefighters work for the fire department.
They put water on burning buildings.

Sanitation workers clean the city streets.

Mail carriers bring letters to our homes.

Use *LWE Illustrations 3*, pp. 40–41.

DRILL: Identification Drill

Using *LWE Illustrations 3*, pp. 40–41, teacher asks, "Who are they?" and "What do they do?" Student replies may vary.

© New Readers Press. All rights reserved.

VOCABULARY: The Use of *both*

Two police officers arrived quickly.
Both of them had guns.

Two books were on the table.
Both of them were open.

Ann and I are going to the movies.
Both of us like to go to the movies.

Use p. 40 of *LWE Illustrations 3* for the police officers, and use actual books. Explain that *both* refers to two.

DRILL: Rejoinder Drill

Teacher makes a statement, to which the student replies using *both*.

Teacher	Student
Gail and Jason painted the chairs. Both of them like to paint.	Both of them like to paint.
Two police officers arrived quickly. Both of them had guns.	Both of them had guns.

Ann and Kim are going to the movies.
Ray and Kay go camping.
Pete and Steve work in the repair shop.
Gail and Jason painted the chairs.
Two police officers arrived quickly.
Fran and Mike were sad that Tom died.
Carla and David went to a dinner party for Carla's class.
You and Ann are good students.

VOCABULARY: Past Participles of Irregular Verbs

break	broke	broken
choose	chose	chosen
drive	drove	driven
freeze	froze	frozen
ride	rode	ridden
steal	stole	stolen

1. Teacher models all three forms of each verb in a sentence as student listens. Explain the meaning of any verbs the student does not understand.

2. Teacher models all three forms of each verb. Student repeats.

© New Readers Press. All rights reserved.

VOCABULARY: Past Participles of Irregular Verbs

Ed broke a glass yesterday.
He has broken many glasses.

Gail chose pink paint.
Gail has chosen many paints.

Pete drove the car very fast.
Pete has driven that car for a long time.

We froze the meat.
We have frozen the meat.

They rode to the bank on the bus.
They have ridden to school with Jason every week.

Someone stole Tony's ring last week.
Someone has stolen my coat.

---

1. Teacher models the sentences in pairs. Student listens.
2. Teacher models the sentences. Student repeats after each sentence.

DRILL: Answering Questions

Teacher asks a question in the present perfect tense which the student answers in the negative.

Teacher	Student
Have you broken anything today? No, I haven't broken anything today.	No, I haven't broken anything today.
Have you chosen a book to read? No, I haven't chosen one.	No, I haven't chosen one.
Have you ever driven a truck?	
Have you frozen the meat?	
Have you ever ridden in a truck?	
Have you ever stolen anything?	
Have you ever broken something in a store?	
Have you chosen a book to read?	

© New Readers Press. All rights reserved.

STRUCTURE FOCUS: The Passive Voice

Active	Passive
Someone steals the ring.	The ring is stolen.
Someone broke the lock.	The lock was broken.

1. Teacher models each pair of sentences, first the active and then the passive.

2. Teacher models each pair of sentences.
   Student repeats the passive sentence.

Note: The passive voice is formed by using the verb *be* and the past participle of the main verb. In the passive, the object of the active verb becomes the subject of the passive verb.

DRILL: Transformation Drill

Teacher gives an active sentence which the student must change to the passive.

Teacher	Student
Someone stole the book. The book was stolen.	The book was stolen.
People speak English in many countries. English is spoken in many countries.	English is spoken in many countries.

Someone wrote this book.
Someone drove the truck.
Someone broke the lock.
Someone stole the book.
People speak English in many countries.

© New Readers Press. All rights reserved.

STRUCTURE FOCUS: Passive Voice with *get*

She	got	tired.
They	are getting	married.
Mrs. Green	got	upset.
They	get	paid at the end of the month.
Nobody	got	hurt.
She	gets	worried when Lee is late.

As you model each sentence, ask the student to listen to *get*.

DRILL: Making Sentences

Teacher gives words which the student must use in a sentence.

Teacher	**Student**
get upset I get upset when I am tired.	I get upset when I am tired.
get tired Ann got tired.	Ann got tired.
get tired get paid get hurt get worried get upset	

STRUCTURE FOCUS: The Use of *can* and *could*

I can speak Italian now.
I could speak Italian when I was a child.

He can play hockey now.
He could play hockey when he was young.

1. Teacher models each pair of sentences, asking the student to listen to *can* and *could.* Student listens.

2. Teacher models the sentences. Student repeats after each sentence.

© New Readers Press. All rights reserved.

STRUCTURE FOCUS: The Use of *could* and *couldn't*

Could you speak English when you were a child?
No, I couldn't.

Could Lee Chan read Chinese when he was young?
Yes, he could.

---

1. Teacher models each question and answer, asking the student to listen to *could* and *couldn't.*

2. Teacher models the sentences. Student repeats after each sentence.

DRILL: Transformation Drill

Teacher gives statement which the student must change to the question form and then answer.

Teacher	**Student**
Fran could not run five miles at first.	
Could Fran run five miles at first?	Could Fran run five miles at first?
No, she couldn't.	No, she couldn't.
Gail and Jason could paint the kitchen.	
Could Gail and Jason paint the kitchen?	Could Gail and Jason paint the kitchen?
Yes, they could.	Yes, they could.

Pete could play hockey when he was young.
Steve could fix radios before he worked for Pete.
Lee Green could pay for the tree.
The police couldn't find Tony's clock radio.
I could speak Spanish when I was young.
I could speak English when I was a child.
Lee Chan could read Chinese when he was a child.

© New Readers Press. All rights reserved.

STRUCTURE FOCUS: *If* Clauses

I can't tell	if he is right.
I can't tell	if anyone is in the room.
We'll see	if anyone can help us.
I'll ask Carla	if she can cook for us.

As you model each sentence, ask the student to listen to *if*.

DRILL: Answering Questions

Teacher asks questions which the student must answer using the words given to begin the sentence.

Teacher	**Student**
Is he right? I can't tell. I can't tell if he is right.	I can't tell if he is right.
Can anyone help us? We'll see. We'll see if anyone can help us.	We'll see if anyone can help us.

Is anyone at home? I can't tell.
Can Carla cook for us? I'll ask Carla.
Does Ed want to watch TV? I'll see.
Is she crying? I can't tell.
Is it raining outside? I can't tell.
Is he right? I can't tell.
Can Jason help us with our homework? I'll ask Jason.
Can anyone help us? We'll see.

© New Readers Press. All rights reserved.

STRUCTURE FOCUS: Clauses with *so*

I am tired,	so I am going to bed.
Ellen's husband died,	so she is very sad.
It was his mother's ring,	so he loved it.

As you model each sentence, ask the student to listen to *so*.

DRILL: Combining Sentences

Teacher gives two sentences which the student must combine using *so*.

Teacher	**Student**
I am tired. I am going to bed. I am tired, so I am going to bed.	I am tired, so I am going to bed.
My TV is broken. I can't watch it. My TV is broken, so I can't watch it.	My TV is broken, so I can't watch it.

It was his mother's ring.
He loved it.

Lee wants to learn English.
He is studying hard.

Ellen's husband died.
She is very sad.

My radio is broken.
Steve is going to fix it.

I'm not hungry.
I'm not going to have dinner.

I am tired.
I am going to bed.

My TV is broken.
I can't watch it.

© New Readers Press. All rights reserved.

LISTENING COMPREHENSION

Tony Romano lived in a big apartment building. One evening, Tony got back to his apartment very late. The door was open, and the lock was broken. He called the police.

Tony looked at his apartment. His sofa was stolen. His TV and clock radio were stolen. A gold ring was missing.

Tony was sad because so many things were stolen.

---

1. Teacher reads the story twice at a normal pace.
   Student listens. Student asks about words he does not know.

2. Student tells the story in his own words. If the student cannot tell the story, teacher may begin the sentence and have the student complete it.

Note: If the student cannot remember the story, read it once or twice again.

ORAL EVALUATION

1. Review the expressions with *Oh* by doing the Rejoinder Drill.
2. Using *LWE Illustrations 3*, pp. 40–41, review the names of public employees.
   Student should know all of them.
3. Review the use of *both* by doing the Rejoinder Drill.
4. Review the past participles of irregular verbs by doing the drill on Answering Questions.
5. Review the passive voice by doing the Transformation Drill.
6. Review the passive with *get* by doing the drill on Making Sentences.
7. Review *if* clauses by doing the drill on Answering Questions.
8. Review the use of *could* by doing the Transformation Drill.
9. Review clauses with *so* by doing the drill on Combining Sentences.

II. Reading and Writing

BOOK 3: Lesson 16

Complete Lesson 16 in book 3, following the instructions given in *Laubach Way to Reading Teacher's Edition 3*. Adapt the wording of the suggested teacher's instructions to the student as needed for your ESL student's comprehension.

ADDITIONAL WRITTEN PRACTICE

After completing Lesson 16 in book 3, have the student do the practices for Lesson 16 in workbook 3.

© New Readers Press. All rights reserved.

Lesson 17

OBJECTIVES

When a student completes this lesson, he should be able to:

1. Say and respond to a new dialog.
2. Say some words about sleepwear.
3. Say some words about bedding.
4. Say the past participle of these irregular verbs: *shake* (*shaken*), *speak* (*spoken*), *take* (*taken*), *wake* (*waked*), *write* (*wrote*).
5. Use *hope* + *that* clause, as in *I hope that it won't rain today.*
6. Use adjective + *that* clause.
7. Use *so* as a substitute in the expressions *I hope so* and *I think so*.
8. Listen to a story and repeat it in his own words.

VISUAL AIDS

Use *LWE Illustrations 3*, pp. 42–43.

I. Conversation Skills

DIALOG

A: This is Rose Jones.
There's a fire in my home.
It's at 1428 Valley Drive.
The fire is in the kitchen.

B: Where are you?
A: I'm phoning from next door.

B: Is anyone in your house?
A: No, but I can't find my dog.

B: Don't worry about the dog.
Don't go back home.
Don't try to save anything.
A: Please hurry.

© New Readers Press. All rights reserved.

VOCABULARY: Sleepwear

Joe wears pajamas to bed.
Rose wears a nightgown to bed.
Joe wears a robe and slippers in the morning.
Rose wears a robe and slippers in the morning.

Use p. 42 of *LWE Illustrations 3* for the new vocabulary.

DRILL: Identification Drill

Using p. 42 of *LWE Illustrations 3*, ask the student, "What's this?" to elicit vocabulary items.

VOCABULARY: Bedding

My bed has a hard mattress.
I put sheets on the mattress.
I put a blanket over the sheets.
I sleep with my head on a pillow.

Use p. 43 of *LWE Illustrations 3* for the new vocabulary.

DRILL: Identification Drill

Using p. 43 of *LWE Illustrations 3*, ask, "What's this?" to elicit the vocabulary items.

© New Readers Press. All rights reserved.

VOCABULARY: Past Participles of Irregular Verbs

shake	shook	shaken
speak	spoke	spoken
take	took	taken
wake	woke	waked
write	wrote	written

1. Teacher models all three forms of each verb.
   Explain any verbs the student does not understand. Student listens.

2. Teacher models all three forms of each verb. Student repeats.

Note: For the past participle of *wake*, the form *woken* is also acceptable. If this is the form you always use, substitute it here and in the following drill.

DRILL: Answering Questions

Teacher asks a question in the present perfect tense which the student answers in the negative.

Teacher	Student
Have you ever spoken to Ellen? No, I have never spoken to Ellen.	No, I have never spoken to Ellen.
Have you ever shaken hands with Mr. Chan? No, I have never shaken hands with Mr. Chan.	No, I have never shaken hands with Mr. Chan.

Have you ever taken a Chinese class?
Have you ever waked up before the sun?
Have you ever written a letter in English?
Have you ever shaken hands with Mr. Chan?
Have you ever spoken to Ellen?

© New Readers Press. All rights reserved.

STRUCTURE FOCUS: *hope* + *that* Clause

I hope that they can save Rose and Joe's house.
I hope that I can go camping for three days.
I hope that it won't rain today.

As you model each sentence, ask the student to listen to *hope*.

DRILL: Making Sentences

Teacher gives words which student must use in a sentence with *I hope that*.

Teacher	Student
It won't rain today. I hope that it won't rain today.	I hope that it won't rain today.
I will see you again. I hope that I will see you again.	I hope that I will see you again.

I have learned my lesson.
I can go camping for three days.
I can get a new winter coat.
The firefighters can save Rose and Joe's house.
Ellen won't be sad.
Fran will win the race.
It won't rain today.
I will see you again.

© New Readers Press. All rights reserved.

STRUCTURE FOCUS: *so* as a Substitute

Do you think it will be sunny today?	I hope so. I think so.
Do you think they will save Rose and Joe's house?	I hope so. I think so.
Do you hope that Fran will win the race?	I hope so. I think so.

1. Teacher models each question and both of its answers, asking the student to listen to *I hope so* and *I think so.* Student listens.

2. Teacher models the question and its answers. Student repeats each answer.

DRILL: Question and Answer Drill

Teacher asks a question which the student answers using *I hope so* or *I think so.*

Teacher	**Student**
Do you think it will rain today? I think so.	I think so.
Do you think Fran will win the race? I hope so.	I hope so.

Do you think Lee will pay for the tree?
Do you think Fran likes to run?
Do you hope that Fran will win the race?
Do you think that the firefighters will save Rose and Joe's house?
Do you think that Jill will be a good driver?

© New Readers Press. All rights reserved.

LISTENING COMPREHENSION

If you have a fire, there are three things to think of: First, get everyone away from the burning building fast. Don't stop to telephone. Don't stop to take anything with you.

Second, phone the fire department from next door or from a pay phone.

Third, never go back into a burning building.

---

1. Teacher reads the story twice at a normal pace.
   Student listens. Student asks about words he does not know.

2. Student tells the story in his own words. If the student cannot tell the story, teacher may begin the sentence and have the student complete it.

Note: If the student cannot remember the story, read it once or twice again.

ORAL EVALUATION

1. Using *LWE Illustrations 3*, pp. 42–43, have the student identify sleepwear and bedding.
   Student should know all of the items.

2. Review the past participle of the irregular verbs by doing the drill on Answering Questions.
   Student should know all of the items.

3. Review *hope* + *that* clauses by doing the drill on Making Sentences.

4. Review *so* as a substitute by doing the Question and Answer Drill.

II. Reading and Writing

BOOK 3: Lesson 17

Complete Lesson 17 in book 3, following the instructions given in the *Laubach Way to Reading Teacher's Edition 3*. Adapt the wording of the suggested teacher's instructions to the student as needed for your ESL student's comprehension.

ADDITIONAL WRITTEN PRACTICE

After completing Lesson 17 in book 3, have the student do the practices for Lesson 17 in workbook 3.

© New Readers Press. All rights reserved.

Lesson 18

OBJECTIVES

When a student completes this lesson, he should be able to:

1. Say and respond to a new dialog.
2. Say the words *map* and *way*.
3. Say some geographical terms.
4. Say some expressions of place.
5. Say the names of the four seasons.
6. Say some words about cooking appliances.
7. Say some words about catching cold.
8. Say some action verbs: *load, lift, push, pull, drop*.
9. Use *which* in questions.
10. Use questions with *Would you mind* + verb-*ing*.
11. Answer questions with *Would you mind?*
12. Use *spend* + time expressions + verb-*ing*.
13. Listen to a story and repeat it in his own words.

VISUAL AIDS

1. *LWE Illustrations 3*, pp. 44–47.
2. The maps on p. 103 and p. 125 of book 3.
3. A globe or world map.
4. Any of these items that it is convenient to bring: a toaster, a frying pan, a can and can opener, a coffee pot, a teapot.

I. Conversation Skills

DIALOG

A: Would you mind opening the door for me?
My hands are full.
B: I'll be glad to.
Can I help you with your packages?

A: Thank you.
Would you take this box and put it on the table?
B: Sure.

© New Readers Press. All rights reserved.

VOCABULARY: *map* and *way*

Look at the map to find Valley Road.
Look at the map to find the way to Green Lake State Park.

Use the map on p. 103 of book 3.

VOCABULARY: Geographical Terms

Ed is standing on the bank of the river.
Jill is standing on the shore of the lake.
Tom is standing on the shore of the ocean.

There is sand at the ocean.
Children play in the sand.
They like a sandy beach.

There is an island in the lake.
There are islands in the ocean.
Cuba is an island.

Use *LWE Illustrations 3*, pp. 44–45, for the first seven sentences.
Use a globe or world map to point to islands in the ocean.
Use the map on p. 125 of book 3 or a globe or world map to show Cuba.

DRILL: Identification Drill

Using the visual aids listed above for the geographical terms, ask questions to elicit the vocabulary items.

VOCABULARY: Expressions of Place

This is the front of the book.
This is the middle of the book.
This is the end of the book.

Use a book to show the meaning of the expressions.

DRILL: Identification Drill

Using the visual aids listed above for the geographical terms, ask questions to elicit the vocabulary items.

© New Readers Press. All rights reserved.

VOCABULARY: The Four Seasons

There are four seasons in the year.
In the winter, it is cold. People go skiing.
In the spring, the trees are green. People go fishing.
In the summer, it is warm. People go swimming.
In the fall, the leaves of the trees get yellow and red.

DRILL: Answering Questions

Teacher asks questions to elicit the vocabulary.

Teacher	Student
How many seasons are there? There are four seasons.	There are four seasons.
When is it cold? It is cold in the winter.	It is cold in the winter.

When are the trees green?
When is it warm?
When is it cold?
When do the leaves of the trees get yellow and red?
How many seasons are there?

VOCABULARY: Cooking Appliances

Joan toasts bread in the toaster.
Joan roasts meat in the oven.
Joan bakes a cake in the oven.
Joan boils water on top of the stove.
Joan fries fish in a frying pan.
She opens a can with a can opener.
She makes coffee in a coffee pot.
She makes tea in a teapot.

Use *LWE Illustrations 3*, pp. 46–47, or actual objects.

© New Readers Press. All rights reserved.

VOCABULARY: Catching Cold

People catch cold in the winter.
When a person has a cold, he has a sore throat.
He sneezes a lot and has to blow his nose.
He needs to drink a lot of water.
He needs to rest in bed.

Act out the meaning of the new vocabulary items.

DRILL: Answering Questions

Teacher asks questions which elicit the vocabulary items. As necessary, act out items to elicit responses (e.g., sneezing, blowing his nose).

Teacher	Student
What do people catch in the winter? They catch cold.	They catch cold.
When a person has a cold, what does he do? (Teacher sneezes.) He sneezes.	He sneezes.
When a person has a cold, what does he do? (Teacher blows her nose.)	
When a person has a cold, what does he have? (Teacher touches her throat and looks uncomfortable.)	
When a person has a cold, what does he need to drink? When a person has a cold, what does he need to do?	

VOCABULARY: Action Verbs

Tom puts boxes in the trunk. He loads the trunk.
He lifts the boxes up.
The box is heavy. He drops it.
He pushes the door shut.
He pulls the door open.

Act out the meaning of the verbs.

DRILL: Answering Questions

Teacher acts out the verbs and asks, "What am I doing?" For example, teacher lifts something and asks, "What am I doing?" Continue with the remaining items.

© New Readers Press. All rights reserved.

STRUCTURE FOCUS: Questions with *Which*

Which dress did you buy?	The blue one.
Which road are you going to take?	The shore road.
Which book did you read?	The English book.
Which coat did you wear?	The black one.

1. Teacher models each question and answer, asking the student to listen to *which*. Student listens.

2. Teacher models each question and answer. Student repeats after each sentence.

DRILL: Making Questions

Teacher gives a statement which the student must put in the question form.

Teacher	**Student**
I bought a blue dress. Which dress did you buy?	Which dress did you buy?
I put the brown bag in the car. Which bag did you put in the car?	Which bag did you put in the car?

She is taking Valley Road.
Ann is reading the English book.
Sam is wearing his black coat.
I bought the blue dress.
They went to Green Lake State Park.
Lee is going to take Flight 406.
Mike packed his black tie.
I put the brown bag in the car.

© New Readers Press. All rights reserved.

STRUCTURE FOCUS: *Would you mind* + Verb-*ing*

Would you mind closing the door?
Would you mind opening the window?
Would you mind putting the bags in the trunk?

As you model each sentence, ask the student to listen to *Would you mind?*

DRILL: Making Questions

Teacher gives words which the student must use in the question form with *Would you mind.* Student completes the question.

Teacher	**Student**
close the window Would you mind closing the window?	Would you mind closing the window?
go by bus Would you mind going by bus?	Would you mind going by bus?

close the window
open the door
give me the book on the table
help me fill out this application
bring a green salad to the party
carry these books for me
put the bags in the trunk

© New Readers Press. All rights reserved.

STRUCTURE FOCUS: Answers to *Would you mind?*

Would you mind closing the window?
Not at all.

Would you mind helping me?
I'd be glad to.

Would you mind bringing a green salad to the party?
I'm sorry, but I'm not going to the party.

---

1. Teacher models each question and answer, asking the student to listen to the answer. Student listens.

2. Teacher models each question and answer. Student repeats the answer.

DRILL: Question and Answer Drill

Teacher asks a question which the student answers using an appropriate reply. Student replies may vary.

Teacher	**Student**
Would you mind going by bus? I'm sorry, but I can't.	I'm sorry, but I can't.
Would you mind helping me? I'd be glad to.	I'd be glad to.

Would you mind putting the bags in the trunk?
Would you mind giving me the book on the table?
Would you mind going by bus?
Would you mind carrying these books for me?
Would you mind helping me fill out this application?
Would you mind closing the window?
Would you mind closing the door?

© New Readers Press. All rights reserved.

STRUCTURE FOCUS: *spend* + Time Expressions + Verb-*ing*

Joan and her mother	spent	the day	fishing.
I	spent	two hours	studying.
Mrs. Oak	spent	an hour	making dinner.

As you model each sentence, ask the student to listen to *spent*.

DRILL: Combining Sentences

Teacher gives two sentences which the student must combine into one sentence.

Teacher	**Student**
I spent two hours. I studied English. I spent two hours studying English.	I spent two hours studying English.
Ed spent the day. He worked. Ed spent the day working.	Ed spent the day working.
Joan and her mother spent the day. They fished.	
The two men spent a lot of time. They talked.	
Joan spent the weekend. She camped.	
Mrs. Oak spent an hour. She made dinner.	
I spent two hours. I watched TV.	
I spent all my time. I listened to the radio.	
I spent two hours. I studied English.	
Ed spent the day. He worked.	

© New Readers Press. All rights reserved.

LISTENING COMPREHENSION

When you go camping in October, you need to take many things with you. You need a tent and a sleeping bag. You need bread and cheese. You can take coffee to drink. You can go fishing and roast the fish over a fire.

Sometimes, it's cold in October, and it rains. You need heavy clothes and a heavy coat.

---

1. Teacher reads the story twice at a normal pace.
   Student listens. Student asks about words he does not know.
2. Student tells the story in his own words. If the student cannot tell the story, teacher may begin the sentence and have the student complete it.

Note: If the student cannot remember the story, read it once or twice again.

ORAL EVALUATION

1. Using *LWE Illustrations 3*, pp. 44–45, and a globe or world map, have the student identify the geographical terms. Student should know 5 of them.
2. Have the student identify the four seasons using the drill on Answering Questions.
3. Using *LWE Illustrations 3*, pp. 46–47, have the student identify names of the cooking appliances. Student should know 8 of them.
4. Review the vocabulary on catching a cold by doing Answering Questions Drill.
5. Review the action verbs by doing the drill on Answering Questions. Student should know 4 of them.
6. Review questions with *which* by doing the drill on Making Questions.
7. Review questions with *Would you mind?* by doing the drill on Making Questions.
8. Review polite replies to *Would you mind?* by doing the Question and Answer Drill.
9. Review *spend* + time expressions + verb-*ing* by doing the drill on Combining Sentences.

II. Reading and Writing

BOOK 3: Lesson 18

Complete Lesson 18 in book 3, following the instructions given in *Laubach Way to Reading Teacher's Edition 3*. Adapt the wording of the suggested teacher's instructions to the student as needed for your ESL student's comprehension.

ADDITIONAL WRITTEN PRACTICE

After completing Lesson 18 in book 3, have the student do the practices for Lesson 18 in workbook 3.

© New Readers Press. All rights reserved.

Lesson 19

OBJECTIVES

When a student completes this lesson, he should be able to:

1. Say and respond to a new dialog.
2. Say some chart and story words about things that happen on the road.
3. Say some words about the weather.
4. Say the words *ahead* and *behind.*
5. Say the expression *back and forth.*
6. Say the irregular verbs *blow, know*, and *throw.*
7. Use *had better.*
8. Use *so* + adjective + *that* clause, as in *It's so dark outside that I can't see.*
9. Listen to a story and repeat it in his own words.

VISUAL AIDS

1. *LWE Illustrations 3*, pp. 48–49.
2. An outdoor thermometer (Fahrenheit).

I. Conversation Skills

DIALOG

A: It's so cold. It's freezing out today.
B: Yes, it's five below zero.

A: And it's windy. That makes it seem colder.
B: Do you like the cold weather?

A: Yes, I do. And I like the snow, too.
B: Why?

A: Because I want to go skiing.
B: That's my favorite winter sport, too.

Use *LWE Illustrations 3*, p. 48.

© New Readers Press. All rights reserved.

VOCABULARY: On the Road

The first car leads the way.
The second car follows.
The cars drive at the speed limit.
The speed limit is 55 miles an hour.
It is against the law to drive faster than the speed limit.

VOCABULARY: Weather and Temperatures

When it's zero outside, it's cold.
When it's below zero, it's very cold.
When it's eighty outside, it's warm.
When it's above eighty, it's very warm.
When it's thirty-two outside, water freezes. It changes to ice.

Use the thermometer in *LWE Illustrations 3*, p. 49, or a real thermometer to show the temperature in each sentence.

VOCABULARY: *ahead* and *behind*

Ed is in front of us. He is ahead.
Joan is in back of us. She is behind.

VOCABULARY: *back and forth*

She rocked back and forth.
The man rocked the car back and forth.
He goes back and forth to work by car.

Demonstrate the meaning of *back and forth* as you model the sentences.

© New Readers Press. All rights reserved.

VOCABULARY: Irregular Verb Forms

blow	blew	have blown
know	knew	have known
throw	threw	have thrown

1. Teacher models all three forms of each verb. Student listens.
2. Teacher models all three forms of each verb. Student repeats.

Note: Act out the meaning of *blow* and *throw*. For example, throw away some paper.

DRILL: Answering Questions

Teacher asks questions which the student answers in the affirmative.

Teacher	**Student**
Did the wind blow hard? Yes, it blew hard.	Yes, it blew hard.
Have you thrown the paper away? Yes, I have thrown it away.	Yes, I have thrown it away.

Does the wind blow snow onto the car windows?
Did he know what to say?
Did Ed throw the paper away?
Has he known Gail for a long time?
Has the wind blown the snow onto the car windows?
Does Sam know how to drive in the snow?
Did the wind blow hard yesterday?

© New Readers Press. All rights reserved.

STRUCTURE FOCUS: The Use of *had better*

I had better take some medicine.	I feel sick.
I'd better take some medicine.	I feel sick.
You had better wear a heavy coat.	It's cold.
You'd better wear a heavy coat.	It's cold.
They had better not drive fast.	It's against the law.
They'd better not drive fast.	It's against the law.

As you model each pair of sentences, ask the student to listen to *had better*, then *I'd better*, and so on.

DRILL: Making Sentences

Teacher gives words which the student must use in sentences beginning with *You'd better*.

Teacher	Student
take some medicine	
You'd better take some medicine.	You'd better take some medicine.
study hard	
You'd better study hard.	You'd better study hard.

wear a heavy coat
drive slowly
not smoke in bed
telephone the police
not drive without a license
take some medicine
study hard

© New Readers Press. All rights reserved.

STRUCTURE FOCUS: *so* + Adjective + *that* Clause

This box is so heavy	that I can't carry it.
I'm so angry	that I could yell.
Ed speaks so softly	that I can't hear him.

As you model each sentence, ask the student to listen to *so ... that.*

Note: The construction *so ... that* is used with an adjective or adverb.

DRILL: Combining Sentences

Teacher gives two sentences which the student combines using *so ... that.*

Teacher	Student
This box is heavy. I can't carry it. This box is so heavy that I can't carry it.	This box is so heavy that I can't carry it.
It's snowing hard. Sam cannot see the road. It's snowing so hard that Sam cannot see the road.	It's snowing so hard that Sam cannot see the road.

It's dark outside.
I can't see.

It's snowing hard.
Sam cannot see the road.

He's going fast.
He will miss the turn.

This sweater is expensive.
I can't buy it.

He's talking softly.
I can't hear him.

Joan is sad.
She wants to cry.

I am angry.
I want to yell.

This box is heavy.
I can't carry it.

© New Readers Press. All rights reserved.

LISTENING COMPREHENSION

It is not easy to drive when it is snowing and the wind is blowing. You must drive slowly in the snow. You must clean the ice and snow from your car windows. It's good to have a bag of sand and a blanket in your car. You can throw sand under the car wheels if your car gets stuck.

---

1. Teacher reads the story twice at a normal pace.
   Student listens. Student asks about words he does not know.
2. Student tells the story in his own words. If the student cannot tell the story, teacher may begin the sentence and have the student complete it.

Note: If the student cannot remember the story, read it once or twice again.

ORAL EVALUATION

1. Have the student say the words about things that happen on the road. He should know all of them.
2. Have the student say the words about weather and temperatures. He should know all of them.
3. Act out the words and have the student say *ahead, behind, back and forth.*
4. Review the irregular verbs by having the student do the drill on Answering Questions. Student should be able to answer all the questions.
5. Review *had better* by having the student do the drill on Making Sentences.
6. Review *so* + adjective + *that* clause by having the student do the drill on Combining Sentences.

II. Reading and Writing

BOOK 3: Lesson 19

Complete Lesson 19 in book 3, following the instructions given in *Laubach Way to Reading Teacher's Edition 3*. Adapt the wording of the suggested teacher's instructions to the student as needed for your ESL student's comprehension.

ADDITIONAL WRITTEN PRACTICE

After completing Lesson 19 in book 3, have the student do the practices for Lesson 19 in workbook 3.

© New Readers Press. All rights reserved.

Lesson 20

OBJECTIVES

When a student completes this lesson, he should be able to:

1. Say and respond to a new dialog.
2. Say vocabulary about clothing.
3. Say the word *directory* and recognize what a telephone directory and a store directory are.
4. Use the irregular verbs *tear, wear, swear*.
5. Use words about location: *across the street, on the corner*, and *next to*.
6. Use the expression *can afford to*.
7. Use the superlative form of adjectives.
8. Use *each other*.
9. Use *every other*, as in *every other day*.
10. Listen to a story and repeat it in his own words.

VISUAL AIDS

1. *LWE Illustrations 3*, pp. 50–51.
2. Lined writing paper.
3. A calendar for any month.
4. A telephone directory.

I. Conversation Skills

DIALOG

A: Could you tell me where I can find the men's department?
B: I'm sorry. I don't know.
Let's look at the store directory.

A: Where is it?
B: On the first floor, near the door.

A: Oh, I see it.
Men's Department. Fourth Floor.
Thanks for your help.
B: Sure. Any time.

© New Readers Press. All rights reserved.

VOCABULARY: Clothing

David and Joan went to a department store.
David wanted a <u>sport</u> <u>shirt</u> with <u>short</u> <u>sleeves</u>.
Joan wanted a <u>blouse</u> with <u>long</u> <u>sleeves</u>.
David wanted a <u>sweater</u>, and Joan did, too.
A salesperson in the men's department showed David some shirts and sweaters.
A salesperson in the women's department showed Joan some blouses and sweaters.

Use *LWE Illustrations 3*, p. 50, to show the clothing.

DRILL: Question and Answer Drill

Teacher asks questions to elicit vocabulary items.

Teacher	Student
What did the salesperson show David? The salesperson showed David some shirts.	The salesperson showed David some shirts.
What did Joan want? She wanted a blouse with long sleeves.	She wanted a blouse with long sleeves.
What did David want? What did the salesperson show David? What did Joan want? What did the salesperson show Joan?	

VOCABULARY: A Directory

A <u>store</u> <u>directory</u> is a sign.
It tells where to find things in a department store.

A <u>telephone</u> <u>directory</u> is a book.
It has people's telephone numbers in it.

Use *LWE Illustrations 3*, top of p. 51, to show a store directory in a department store. Show the student the telephone directory you have brought, and point out your own name and number, or the student's, or some other listing that would be meaningful to him.

© New Readers Press. All rights reserved.

VOCABULARY: Irregular Verb Forms

tear	tore	torn
wear	wore	worn
swear	swore	sworn

1. Teacher models all three forms of each verb. Student listens.
2. Teacher models all three forms of each verb. Student repeats.

Note: Explain the meaning of the verbs by *tearing* a piece of paper, making a sentence about some article of clothing you *wear*, and holding up your hand as if taking an oath for *swear.*

DRILL: Answering Questions

Teacher asks a question which the student answers in the affirmative.

Teacher	**Student**
What did she wear? She wore a white blouse.	She wore a white blouse.
What did she tear? She tore some paper.	She tore some paper.

Has she worn that blouse before?
Do you wear hats?
Has he ever torn his shirt?
What did you swear to do?
What did Sam tear?
Have you ever sworn to do something?

VOCABULARY: Expressions of Location

The bookstore is on the corner of York Street and Main Street.
The bookstore is across the street from the post office.
The bank is next to the post office.

Use the map on the bottom of p. 51, *LWE Illustrations 3*, to indicate the locations.

After modeling the sentences and having the student repeat, ask questions with "Where is ...?" to elicit *on the corner of, across the street from,* and *next to.*

© New Readers Press. All rights reserved.

VOCABULARY: *in order* and *out of order*

Steve fixed the TV.	It's in order.
The radio is broken.	It's out of order.

VOCABULARY: *can afford to*

I have enough money.	I can afford to buy these shoes.
I don't have enough money.	I can't afford to buy this car.

As you model each pair of sentences, ask the student to listen to *can afford to* or *can't afford to.*

DRILL: Making Statements

Teacher asks student to tell what he can afford to buy and what he cannot afford to buy. Teacher may begin by telling what she can and cannot afford and having the student repeat these statements.

Teacher	**Student**
I can afford to buy an English book.	I can afford to buy an English book.
I can't afford to buy a new car.	I can't afford to buy a new car.

What can you afford?
What else can you afford?

What can't you afford?
What else can't you afford?

© New Readers Press. All rights reserved.

STRUCTURE FOCUS: Superlatives of Adjectives

He looked at three shirts. He wanted the cheapest one.
The yellow shirt was the best shirt.
The best shirt cost the most money.

As you model each sentence, ask the student to listen to *the cheapest, the best*, and *the most.*

DRILL: Making Questions

Teacher gives words which the student must use with *Which is* to form a question.

Teacher	**Student**
the cheapest shirt Which is the cheapest shirt?	Which is the cheapest shirt?
the most expensive blouse Which is the most expensive blouse?	Which is the most expensive blouse?
the most money the most expensive blouse the cheapest shirt the best blouse the cleanest room the best cake	

© New Readers Press. All rights reserved.

STRUCTURE FOCUS: The Use of *each other*

We write to each other every week.
They see each other every day.
Ann and I telephone each other every morning.

As you model each sentence, ask the student to listen to *each other*.

DRILL: Making Sentences

Teacher gives words which the student must use in a sentence with *each other*.

Teacher	Student
Ann and I write Ann and I write to each other every week.	Ann and I write to each other every week.
We ask We ask each other questions.	We ask each other questions.

We visit
They love
Gail and Jason love
We write
They see
Ann and I telephone

© New Readers Press. All rights reserved.

STRUCTURE FOCUS: The Use of *every other*

Please write on every other line.
He calls me every other day.
Every other street is one-way.

As you model each sentence, ask the student to listen to *every other*.
Use lined paper to demonstrate writing on every other line.
On a calendar, indicate every other day.

DRILL: Answering Questions

Teacher asks questions which the student must answer using *every other*.
Answers may vary.

Teacher	Student
When does he call you? He calls me every other day.	He calls me every other day.
When do you go camping? We go camping every other week.	We go camping every other week.
When does Ed write his mother?	
When does Gail go shopping?	
When does Sam call his friend?	
When does he write?	
When do you go camping?	
When do you go to the movies?	

LISTENING COMPREHENSION

Steve hurried into Porter's Department Store. He looked at the directory on the first floor. He wanted to buy a man's sport shirt. The directory said the men's department was on the fourth floor. Steve hurried to the fourth floor to look at sport shirts. He saw a nice yellow one that he liked very much. He bought it and left the store.

1. Teacher reads the story twice at a normal pace.
   Student listens. Student asks about words he does not know.
2. Student tells the story in his own words. If the student cannot tell the story, teacher may begin the sentence and have the student complete it.

Note: If the student cannot remember the story, read it once or twice again.

© New Readers Press. All rights reserved.

ORAL EVALUATION

1. Have the student do the Question and Answer Drill about clothing. He should be able to answer all the questions.
2. Review the irregular verbs by having the student do the drill on Answering Questions. Student should know all the verb forms.
3. Have the student make three or four sentences telling what he can or cannot afford to buy.
4. Review the superlatives by doing the drill on Making Questions.
5. Review *each other* by doing the drill on Making Sentences.
6. Review *every other* by doing the drill on Answering Questions.

II. Reading and Writing

BOOK 3: Lesson 20

Complete Lesson 20 in book 3, following the instructions given in *Laubach Way to Reading Teacher's Edition 3*. Adapt the wording of the suggested teacher's instructions to the student as needed for your ESL student's comprehension.

ADDITIONAL WRITTEN PRACTICE

After completing Lesson 20 in book 3, have the student do the practices for Lesson 20 in workbook 3.

© New Readers Press. All rights reserved.

Lesson 21

OBJECTIVES

When a student completes this lesson, he should be able to:

1. Say and respond to a new dialog.
2. Use the word *instead.*
3. Use the irregular verbs *come, become, get*, and *forget.*
4. Use vocabulary concerning schools.
5. Use *as far as* and *until.*
6. Use two-word verbs with *up: drink up, eat up, finish up*, and *clean up.*
7. Use *but ... anyway*, as in *She doesn't like TV, but she watches it anyway.*
8. Use *although* clauses.
9. Listen to a story and repeat it in his own words.

VISUAL AIDS

None.

I. Conversation Skills

DIALOG

Gas station attendant:	May I help you?
Customer:	Yes, fill it up with unleaded gas.
Gas station attendant:	All right. Do you want me to check the oil?
Customer:	No, but could you clean my windows?
Gas station attendant:	Sure.
Customer:	How much do I owe you?
Gas station attendant:	Ten dollars, please.

Note: The dialog can be varied by substituting other items or services one can get at a gas station, such as air in tires.

© New Readers Press. All rights reserved.

VOCABULARY: The Use of *instead*

Joe wanted to smoke. He ate instead.
Mary wanted to go shopping. She studied instead.
Tom wanted to buy a yellow shirt. He got a blue one instead.

As you model each pair of sentences, ask the student to listen to *instead.*

DRILL: Question and Answer Drill

Teacher asks questions to elicit *instead.* Student replies may vary.

Teacher	**Student**
Tom wanted to go home. Where did he go instead? He went shopping instead.	He went shopping instead.
Tom wanted to buy a yellow shirt. What did he get instead? He got a blue shirt instead.	He got a blue shirt instead.
Joe wanted to smoke. What did he do instead?	
Ann wanted to go fishing. Where did she go instead?	
Joan wanted to study English. What did she study instead?	
Fran wanted to run. What did she do instead?	
Ann wanted to study. What did she do instead?	

© New Readers Press. All rights reserved.

VOCABULARY: Irregular Verb Forms

come	came	have come
become	became	have become
get	got	have gotten
forget	forgot	have forgotten

1. Teacher models all three forms of each verb. Student listens.
2. Teacher models all three forms of each verb. Student repeats.

DRILL: Answering Questions

Teacher asks a question which the student answers. Student replies may vary.

Teacher	**Student**
When does Ann come to class? She comes to class every day.	She comes to class every day.
What has Fran become? She has become a fast runner.	She has become a fast runner.

When did the police officers come to Tony's house?
Why did you come here?
What has Fran become?
What did Pete become?
What did Ed get?
When did you forget your book?
What have you forgotten?

© New Readers Press. All rights reserved.

VOCABULARY: Schools

Many people go to school.

Young children go to kindergarten first,
then to elementary school.

Teenagers go to junior high school,
then to high school.

After high school, many young people go
to a university or college.

Many adults go to school at night.

DRILL: Question and Answer Drill

Teacher asks questions to elicit vocabulary items.

Teacher	**Student**
Where do children go to school first? They go to kindergarten.	They go to kindergarten.
After kindergarten, where do children go to school? They go to elementary school.	They go to elementary school.

Who goes to school?
Where do children go to school first?
Where do children go after kindergarten?
Where do teenagers go to school?
After high school, where do many young people go to school?
When do many adults go to school?

© New Readers Press. All rights reserved.

VOCABULARY: *as far as* and *until*

He walked as far as the lake.
Ed came as far as the park.

He studied until 10 o'clock.
He lived in Canada until 1980.

As you model each sentence, ask the student to listen to *as far as* or *until.*

Note: *As far as* is used with a place, whereas *until* is used with a time.

DRILL: Question and Answer Drill

Teacher asks a question which the student answers using *as far as* or *until.* Student replies may vary.

Teacher	Student
How far did Tony walk? He walked as far as the lake.	He walked as far as the lake.
How long did Carla study? She studied until 10 o'clock.	She studied until 10 o'clock.

How far did Fran run?
How far did Pete walk with you?
How long did Rosa work?
How long did Pete live in Canada?
How long did Carla study English?

© New Readers Press. All rights reserved.

VOCABULARY: Two-Word Verbs with *up*

Drink up your milk.	Don't leave any in the glass.
Eat up your meat.	Don't leave any on the plate.
Finish up your homework.	Do all the homework.
Clean up your room.	Don't leave it dirty.

1. Teacher models each pair of sentences, asking the student to listen to *drink up, eat up, finish up*, and *clean up*. Student listens.
2. Teacher models the sentence. Student repeats after each sentence.

Note: The use of *up* emphasizes doing the action to its final point.

DRILL: Making Sentences

Teacher gives words or phrases which the student uses in statements with *drink up, eat up, finish up*, and *clean up*. Student replies may vary.

Teacher	**Student**
your room Clean up your room.	Clean up your room.
the letter Finish up the letter.	Finish up the letter.
the milk	
the meat on your plate	
your homework	
your room	
the kitchen	
this job	

© New Readers Press. All rights reserved.

STRUCTURE FOCUS: The Use of *but ... anyway*

She doesn't like TV,	but she watches it anyway.
It was raining,	but they went camping anyway.
Steve was very busy,	but he fixed Mrs. Green's radio anyway.

As you model each sentence, ask the student to listen to *but ... anyway*.

DRILL: Combining Sentences

Teacher gives sentences which the student combines using *but ... anyway*.

Teacher	Student
She doesn't like TV. She watches it. She doesn't like TV, but she watches it anyway.	She doesn't like TV, but she watches it anyway.
There was ice on the road. He drove fast. There was ice on the road, but he drove fast anyway.	There was ice on the road, but he drove fast anyway.
It was raining. They went camping.	
This coat is old. I'm going to wear it.	
It's late. I'm going to call Joan.	
Meat is expensive. We buy it.	
Steve was busy. He fixed Mrs. Green's radio.	
Steve tore his shirt. He wore it.	
He should study. He is going to the movies.	

© New Readers Press. All rights reserved.

STRUCTURE FOCUS: *Although* Clauses

Although she was tired, she went to work.
Although it was cold, Tony went fishing.
Although it was late, Mrs. Green wasn't sleeping.

As you model each sentence, ask the student to listen to *although*.

DRILL: Combining Sentences

Teacher gives sentences which the student must combine using *although*.

Teacher	**Student**
Rose was tired. She went to work. Although Rose was tired, she went to work.	Although Rose was tired, she went to work.
The police tried hard. They didn't find Tony's sofa. Although the police tried hard, they didn't find Tony's sofa.	Although the police tried hard, they didn't find Tony's sofa.
Lee's car hit the tree. He did not get hurt.	
Rose was tired. She went to work.	
It was cold. Joan went swimming.	
Pete wanted to play hockey. He had to get another job.	
Steve was busy. He fixed the radio.	
It was late. Mrs. Green wasn't sleeping.	

© New Readers Press. All rights reserved.

LISTING COMPREHENSION

Many people enjoy shopping. They like to go shopping on the weekends. They go in many stores to see what is for sale. They go shopping for clothes, for furniture, and for many other things. Although people can't afford to buy everything they want, they have fun looking at the things in the stores. And they buy what they can afford.

---

1. Teacher reads the story twice at a normal pace.
   Student listens. Student asks about words he does not know.
2. Student tells the story in his own words. If the student cannot tell the story, teacher may begin the sentence and have the student complete it.

Note: If the student cannot remember the story, read it once or twice again.

ORAL EVALUATION

1. Have the student do the Question and Answer Drill on *instead.*
2. Review the irregular verbs by doing the drill on Answering Questions.
   Student should know all of the verb forms.
3. Have the student do the Question and Answer Drill on schools.
   Student should be able to answer 4 out of 6 questions.
4. Have student distinguish between *as far as* and *until* by doing the Question and Answer Drill.
5. Have the student make sentences with the two-word verbs with *up*. Student should know all 4 verbs.
6. Have the student do the drill on Combining Sentences using *but ... anyway.*
7. Have the student do the drill on Combining Sentences using *although.*

II. Reading and Writing

BOOK 3: Lesson 21

Complete Lesson 21 in book 3, following the instructions given in *Laubach Way to Reading Teacher's Edition 3.* Adapt the wording of the suggested teacher's instructions to the student as needed for your ESL student's comprehension.

ADDITIONAL WRITTEN PRACTICE

After completing Lesson 21 in book 3, have the student do the practices for Lesson 21 in workbook 3.

© New Readers Press. All rights reserved.

Lesson 22

OBJECTIVES

When a student completes this lesson, he should be able to:

1. Say and respond to a new dialog.
2. Use *wait on* and *wait for*.
3. Use some words about time: *present, past, future*.
4. Use some words about restaurants.
5. Name some musical instruments.
6. Use the word *union* in the sense of a labor union.
7. Use the words *citizen, immigrant*, and *refugee*.
8. Say the directions: *north, east, south*, and *west*.
9. Identify the directions on a map.
10. Say the names of some states and identify which part of the country (North, East, South, West) they are in.
11. Name some countries and people of North America.
12. Use *look forward to* + nouns.
13. Use *look forward to* + verb-*ing*.
14. Listen to a story and repeat it in his own words.

VISUAL AIDS

1. *LWE Illustrations 3*, pp. 52–53.
2. A calendar for a year.
3. Map on p. 125 of book 3.

I. Conversation Skills

DIALOG

A: Do you like to listen to music?
B: Yes, I like music.
I listen to music on the radio all the time.

A: What kind of music do you like?
B: I like fast music and some slow songs, too.

A: Do you play in a band?
B: No, I don't. I just like to listen.

Note: The dialog can be varied by discussing the kinds of music the student likes.

© New Readers Press. All rights reserved.

VOCABULARY: *wait on* and *wait for*

Rosa waits on tables at the snack shop.
The flight attendant waits on the passengers on the plane.

Ann is late. I'm waiting for her.
Ed is coming at 8 o'clock. We'll wait for him.

As you model the sentences, ask the student to listen to *wait on* and *wait for*.

Note: *Wait on* is used to mean "serve," whereas *wait for* means "to stay or remain until something happens."

DRILL: Question and Answer Drill

Teacher asks questions to elicit answers with *wait on* and *wait for*.

Teacher	Student
What does Rosa do at the snack shop? She waits on tables.	She waits on tables.
Ann is late. What are you going to do? I'm going to wait for her.	I'm going to wait for her.
The teacher isn't here yet. What are you going to do? What does the flight attendant do? What does the waiter do? Ann is late. What are you going to do? Hugo isn't here yet. What are you going to do?	

VOCABULARY: Words about Time

Today is the present.
Yesterday was the past.
Tomorrow is the future.

DRILL: Answering Questions

Using a calendar, point to the day the class is in session. Say, "This is the present."

Point to other dates to elicit the sentences *This is the future* and *This is the past*. Conclude by pointing again to the present date to elicit *This is the present*.

© New Readers Press. All rights reserved.

VOCABULARY: Restaurants

Gail and Jason went to a restaurant for dinner.
They looked at the menu to see what to eat.

There were many desserts on the menu.
There was cake, apple pie, and ice cream.

There were many beverages on the menu.
There was milk, coffee, tea, and soda.

Use *LWE Illustrations 3*, top of p. 52.

DRILL: Question and Answer Drill

Teacher asks questions to elicit vocabulary items.

Teacher	Student
Where did Gail and Jason go for dinner? They went to a restaurant.	They went to a restaurant.
What did they look at in the restaurant? They looked at the menu.	They looked at the menu.

Why did Gail and Jason look at the menu?
Where did Gail and Jason go for dinner?
What were some of the desserts on the menu?
What were some of the beverages on the menu?

VOCABULARY: Musical Instruments

Hugo plays in a band with other people.
Ann plays the piano.
Hugo plays the drums.
Ed plays the guitar.

Use *LWE Illustrations 3*, bottom of p. 52.

DRILL: Identification Drill

Teacher points to the picture on p. 52 of *LWE Illustrations 3*, and asks questions to elicit the vocabulary, such as: "What does Hugo play in?" "What's this?" and "What does _____ play?"

© New Readers Press. All rights reserved.

VOCABULARY: *join a union*

Ed joined a union when he worked at a car factory.
Hugo joined a union when he wanted to play in a band.
Many people who work belong to unions.
They are union members.

VOCABULARY: *citizens, immigrants,* and *refugees*

The people of a country are its citizens.
Immigrants are people who move into a new country to live.
Refugees are people who leave their country because they are afraid.

VOCABULARY: Directions

In the morning, the sun comes up in the east.
In the afternoon, the sun is in the south.
In the evening, the sun goes down in the west.
The sun is never in the north.

As you model each sentence, ask the student to listen to *east, south,* and so on. Point to the actual direction as you say each sentence. You may want to place signs with these words on them around the room.

DRILL: Giving Answers

Teacher elicits the vocabulary. Point to the actual direction for each item, and have the student point also.

Teacher	**Student**
Tell me where the sun comes up in the morning.	
The sun comes up in the east in the morning.	The sun comes up in the east in the morning.
Tell me where the sun is in the afternoon.	
The sun is in the south in the afternoon.	The sun is in the south in the afternoon.

Tell me where the sun comes up in the morning.
Tell me where the sun is in the afternoon.
Tell me where the sun goes down in the evening.
Tell me where the sun never is.

© New Readers Press. All rights reserved.

VOCABULARY: Directions on a Map

This is a map.
This is north.
This is east.
This is south.
This is west.

Use the map on p. 53 of *LWE Illustrations 3* to indicate the directions.
After you have modeled the sentences and have had the student repeat, indicate the various directions, and have the student identify them.

VOCABULARY: States and Directions

This is a map of the United States.
There are 50 states in the United States.

New York is in the East.
Florida is in the South.
Texas is in the South.
California is in the West.
Minnesota is in the North.

Use the map on p. 53 of *LWE Illustrations 3* again.

DRILL: Question and Answer Drill

Teacher asks questions to elicit the vocabulary.

Teacher	**Student**
Where is New York? New York is in the East.	New York is in the East.
Where is Minnesota? Minnesota is in the North.	Minnesota is in the North.
Where is Texas? Where is California? Where is Minnesota? Where is Florida? Where is New York?	

© New Readers Press. All rights reserved.

VOCABULARY: Countries in North America

The United States, Mexico, and Canada are
big countries in North America.

Cuba is a small country in North America.

Cuba and Mexico are south of the United States.
Canada is north of the United States.
Mexico is west of Cuba.
Cuba is east of Mexico.

Use the map on p. 125 of book 3.

DRILL: Answering Questions

Teacher asks questions to elicit vocabulary.
Use the map on p. 125 of book 3.

Teacher	Student
Where is the United States? The United States is in North America.	The United States is in North America.
What are three big countries in North America? The United States, Mexico, and Canada are three big countries in North America.	The United States, Mexico, and Canada are three big countries in North America.

Where is Cuba?
Where is Canada?
Is Canada north of the United States?
Is Cuba west of Mexico?
Is Mexico west of Cuba?
What is a small country in North America?

© New Readers Press. All rights reserved.

VOCABULARY: Some People of North America

Americans live in the United States.
Mexicans live in Mexico.
Canadians live in Canada.
Cubans live in Cuba.

Use the map on p. 125 of book 3.

DRILL: Question and Answer Drill

Teacher asks questions to elicit vocabulary items.

Teacher	**Student**
Where is the United States? It is in North America.	It is in North America.
Who lives in the United States? Americans live in the United States.	Americans live in the United States.

Where is Mexico?
Who lives in Mexico?
Where is Canada?
Who lives in Canada?
Where is Cuba?
Who lives in Cuba?
Which is the biggest country in North America, Canada or the United States?
Which is bigger, Mexico or Cuba?

© New Readers Press. All rights reserved.

STRUCTURE FOCUS: *look forward to* + Noun

The Garcias	look	forward to	a better future.
I'm	looking	forward to	the party on Friday night.

As you model each sentence, ask the student to listen to *look forward to.*

DRILL: Answering Questions

Teacher gives a question and cue which the student must answer using *look forward to* + a noun.

Teacher	**Student**
What are you looking forward to? (the party) I'm looking forward to the party.	I'm looking forward to the party.
What are the Garcias looking forward to? (a better future) The Garcias are looking forward to a better future.	The Garcias are looking forward to a better future.

What is Carla looking forward to?
(the class party)

What is Jill looking forward to?
(her birthday)

What is Fran looking forward to?
(the race)

What is David looking forward to?
(dinner with Carla)

What are the Garcias looking forward to?
(a better future)

What are you looking forward to?
(the party)

© New Readers Press. All rights reserved.

STRUCTURE FOCUS: *look forward to* + Verb-*ing*

They	look	forward	to	going home.
I	look	forward	to	seeing you again.
The Garcias	are looking	forward	to	becoming citizens.

As you model each sentence, ask the student to listen to *look forward to.*

DRILL: Making Questions

Teacher gives words which the student must use with *Are you looking forward to* to form a question.

Teacher	Student
go to the party Are you looking forward to going to the party?	Are you looking forward to going to the party?
see Gail and Jason again Are you looking forward to seeing Gail and Jason again?	Are you looking forward to seeing Gail and Jason again?
get your driver's license	
go to Mexico	
become a citizen	
learn to read English	
go camping next weekend	
play cards with the Masons	

LISTENING COMPREHENSION

The United States, Mexico, and Canada are three big countries in North America, but Canada is the biggest of the three. Mexico and Canada are neighbors of the United States.

Many people in Canada speak English and French. Many people in Mexico speak Spanish and English. Most people in the United States speak English. Some speak a second language.

1. Teacher reads the story twice at a normal pace.
   Student listens. Student asks about words he does not know.
2. Student tells the story in his own words. If the student cannot tell the story, teacher may begin the sentence and have the student complete it.

Note: If the student cannot remember the story, read it once or twice again.

© New Readers Press. All rights reserved.

ORAL EVALUATION

1. Have the student do the drill for *wait on* and *wait for*.
2. Using a calendar, have the student make sentences using *present, past*, and *future*.
3. Have the student do the Question and Answer Drill on restaurants. Student should know all the items.
4. Using *LWE Illustrations 3*, p. 52, have the student identify the musical instruments. Also, ask, "What does Hugo play in?"
5. Using p. 53 of *LWE Illustrations 3*, have the student identify the directions on the map. Also, do the Question and Answer Drill on states and directions.
6. Using the map on p. 125 of *Skill Book 3*, have the student identify some countries in North America and the names of the people of these countries.
7. Have the student review *look forward to* with nouns and with verb-*ing* by doing the two drills.

II. Reading and Writing

BOOK 3: Lesson 22

Complete Lesson 22 in book 3, following the instructions given in *Laubach Way to Reading Teacher's Edition 3*. Adapt the wording of the suggested teacher's instructions to the student as needed for your ESL student's comprehension.

ADDITIONAL WRITTEN PRACTICE

After completing Lesson 22 in book 3, have the student do the practices for Lesson 22 in workbook 3.

© New Readers Press. All rights reserved.

Lesson 23-A

Note: Lessons 23 and 24 are divided into A and B sections, as are Lessons 23 and 24 in book 3. Each section accompanies one story in the correlated reader *Changes*. Because the reading and writing portion of these lessons is very long, dialogs, listening comprehension, and oral evaluations are omitted from the conversation skills portions.

OBJECTIVES

When a student completes this lesson, he should be able to:

1. Use the verb *share*.
2. Use the adjectives *free, expensive*, and *cheap*.
3. Use the verbs *agree* and *disagree*.
4. Use *so* + adjective + *that* clause (review).
5. Use *wonder* + *if* clause.

VISUAL AIDS

None.

I. Conversation Skills

VOCABULARY: The Verb *share*

I pay half of the rent.
Jason pays half of the rent.
We share the cost of the rent.

I did half of the work.
Jason did half of the work.
We shared the work.

1. Teacher models each group of sentences, asking the student to listen to *share*. Student listens.
2. Teacher models each group of sentences. Student repeats sentence with *share*.

© New Readers Press. All rights reserved.

VOCABULARY: *free, expensive, cheap*

This doesn't cost anything.	It's free.
This costs a lot of money.	It's expensive.
This doesn't cost much money.	It's cheap.

1. Teacher models each pair of sentences. Student listens.
2. Teacher models each pair of sentences. Student repeats the sentence with the adjective.

DRILL: Rejoinder Drill

Teacher gives a statement to which the student adds a rejoinder with *free, expensive*, or *cheap*.

Teacher	**Student**
This doesn't cost anything. It's free.	It's free.
This costs a lot of money. This doesn't cost much money. This doesn't cost anything.	

VOCABULARY: The Verbs *agree* and *disagree*

I like music, but Jane doesn't.	We disagree.
I like TV, and Jane does, too.	We agree.

As you model the sentences, ask the student to listen to *agree* and *disagree*.

DRILL: Rejoinder Drill

Teacher tells about two people. Student must say whether they agree or disagree.

Teacher	**Student**
Jason likes ice cream, and Gail does, too. They agree.	They agree.
Jason likes cake, but Gail doesn't. They disagree.	They disagree.
I like to watch TV, and Gail does, too. Kay likes to play cards, and Ray does, too. Carla doesn't like diet soda, but David does. I like to visit Canada, and my friend does, too. Ann likes dogs, but the Smiths don't. Mike likes to fly, and Fran does, too.	

© New Readers Press. All rights reserved.

STRUCTURE FOCUS: Review of *so* + Adjective + *that* Clause

Jason was so	tired	that	he went to sleep.
The dress was so	cheap	that	I wanted it.
It was so	cold	that	I put on my sweater.

As you model each sentence, ask the student to listen to *so ... that.*

DRILL: Combining Sentences

Teacher gives two sentences which the student combines using *so ... that.*

Teacher	**Student**
Jason was very tired. He went to sleep. Jason was so tired that he went to sleep.	Jason was so tired that he went to sleep.
The dress was very cheap. I wanted it. The dress was so cheap that I wanted it.	The dress was so cheap that I wanted it.
It was very cold. I put on my sweater.	
Jason was very busy. He didn't have time to spend with Gail.	
Fran is very sad. She is crying.	
Ed is very angry. He is shouting.	
David is very happy. He is smiling.	

© New Readers Press. All rights reserved.

STRUCTURE FOCUS: *wonder* + *if* Clause

Jason wonders if he will be a good father.
Gail wonders if she can afford a new dress.
I wonder if it will rain this afternoon.

As you model each sentence, ask the student to listen to *wonder if.*

DRILL: Completing Sentences

Teacher begins a sentence which the student completes. Answers may vary.

Teacher	Student
I wonder if Gail	
I wonder if Gail will buy a new dress.	I wonder if Gail will buy a new dress.
I wonder if it	
I wonder if it will rain.	I wonder if it will rain.
Jason wonders if he	
Gail wonders if she	
I wonder if I	
I wonder if it	
Fran wonders if she	
Lee Chan wonders if he	

ORAL EVALUATION

1. Review the adjectives *free, expensive*, and *cheap* by doing the Rejoinder Drill.
2. Have the student do the Rejoinder Drill on *agree* and *disagree.*
3. Review *so* + adjective + *that* clause by doing the drill on Combining Sentences.
4. Review *wonder* + *if* clauses by doing the drill on Completing Sentences.

II. Reading and Writing

BOOK 3: Lesson 23-A

Complete Lesson 23-A in book 3, following the instructions given in *Laubach Way to Reading Teacher's Edition 3*. Adapt the wording of the suggested teacher's instructions to the student as needed for your ESL student's comprehension.

Note: In workbook 3, all of the exercises for Lesson 23 should be done following Lesson 23-B.

© New Readers Press. All rights reserved.

Lesson 23-B

OBJECTIVES

When a student completes this lesson, he should be able to:

1. Use some vocabulary about farm workers.
2. Say some adjectives and their opposites: *hard-working, lazy, friendly, unfriendly, lovely, handsome,* and *ugly*.
3. Use the verb *train*.
4. Use *no* as a modifier of nouns, as in *I have no money*, contrasted with contractions of *not*, as in *I don't have any money*.
5. Use clauses with *so that* to express purpose, as in *I must take classes so that I can get a better job*.
6. Use adjective clauses with *where* and *when*.

VISUAL AIDS

1. *LWE Illustrations 3*, p. 54.
2. A piece of cotton cloth or some item made of cotton.

I. Conversation Skills

VOCABULARY: Farm Workers

Many farm workers are migrant workers.
The migrants go from one farm to another to work.
They pick the crops on the farm.
They pick cotton, peaches, beans, and other fruits and vegetables.

Use *LWE Illustrations 3*, p. 54, which shows migrant workers picking cotton. Also, show the cotton item you brought to help explain the meaning.

© New Readers Press. All rights reserved.

VOCABULARY: Adjective Opposites

Carlos is hard-working. He works very hard.
Ed is lazy. He doesn't work very hard.

Carlos is friendly. He is nice to people.
Ed is unfriendly. He is not nice to people.

That woman is lovely. She looks pretty.
That man is handsome. He looks good, too.
That building is ugly. It looks bad.

As you model each group of sentences, ask the student to listen to *hard-working, lazy*, and so on. Have the student repeat the group of sentences.

DRILL: Answering Questions

Teacher asks questions which elicit the adjectives being taught.

Teacher	**Student**
What do we call a person who works hard? He's hard-working.	He's hard-working.
What do we call a building that looks bad? It's ugly.	It's ugly.

What do we call a person who is nice to people?
What do we call a person who is not nice to people?

What do we call a person who works hard?
What do we call a person who doesn't work very hard?

What do we call a woman who looks pretty?
What do we call a man who looks good?
What do we call a building that looks bad?

© New Readers Press. All rights reserved.

VOCABULARY: The Verb *train*

Fran wants to win the mile race.
She has to <u>train</u> for the race.

Joan wants to be a nurse.
She has to <u>train</u> to become a nurse.

As you model each pair of sentences, ask the student to listen to *train*.

DRILL: Question and Answer Drill

Teacher asks questions which elicit the verb *train*.

Teacher	**Student**
What does Fran have to do to win the race? She has to train for the race.	She has to train for the race.
What does Joan have to do to become a nurse? She has to train to become a nurse.	She has to train to become a nurse.

What does Steve have to do to work in a repair shop?
What does Joan have to do to become a nurse?
What does Fran have to do to win the race?

© New Readers Press. All rights reserved.

STRUCTURE FOCUS: The Use of *no* + Nouns

I have <u>no</u> money.
He had <u>no</u> home of his own.
There was <u>no</u> food in the house.

As you model each sentence, ask the student to listen to *no*.

DRILL: Transformation Drill

Teacher gives statements which the student must change using *no* + nouns.

Teacher	Student
I have money. I have no money.	I have no money.
There is food in the kitchen. There is no food in the kitchen.	There is no food in the kitchen.
He had a home of his own.	
I need help.	
There is a way to help him.	
I have time.	
They have money.	

© New Readers Press. All rights reserved.

STRUCTURE FOCUS: *no* + Nouns, *not* + Verbs

I have no money.	I don't have any money.
There was no food.	There wasn't any food.

1. Teacher models the sentences in pairs, the one with *no* and the one with *not* (contracted). Ask the student to listen to *no* and *not*.
2. Teacher models each pair of sentences. Student repeats after each sentence.

Note: While *no* is used before nouns, *not* is used to make a verb negative. It is often contracted.

DRILL: Transformation Drill

Teacher gives an affirmative sentence which the student must change in two ways to give a negative meaning: once with *no* and once with *not*.

Teacher	**Student**
Gail has some shampoo.	
Gail has no shampoo.	Gail has no shampoo.
Gail doesn't have any shampoo.	Gail doesn't have any shampoo.
I have money.	
I have no money.	I have no money.
I don't have any money.	I don't have any money.
Jason had lunch.	
We have hamburger.	
Carlos had a home of his own.	
I had time to think.	
I put sugar in the tea.	
There is food in the kitchen.	
There are vegetables in the refrigerator.	
There was a way to help Ed.	

© New Readers Press. All rights reserved.

STRUCTURE FOCUS: Clauses with *so that*

I must take classes so that I can get a better job.
She is learning to drive so that she can get a driver's license.

As you model each sentence, ask the student to listen to *so that.*

Note: *So that* is used in cause-and-effect clauses. It is often used with *can* to express ability.

DRILL: Combining Sentences

Teacher gives two sentences which the student combines using *so that.*

Teacher	**Student**
I must take classes. I can get a better job. I must take classes so that I can get a better job.	I must take classes so that I can get a better job.
Lee Chan is in the United States. He can go to the university. Lee Chan is in the United States so that he can go to the university.	Lee Chan is in the United States so that he can go to the university.
Fran runs every day. She can win the mile race.	
They are studying English. They can get better jobs.	
Lee Chan is in the United States. He can go to the university.	
She is learning how to drive. She can get a driver's license.	
They are coming to the United States. They can have a better future.	

© New Readers Press. All rights reserved.

STRUCTURE FOCUS: Adjective Clauses with *where* and *when*

The farm was 200 miles from the city where Carlos lived.
The building where he lives is in the city.

This is the day when I start my English class.
Monday is the day when I will see Hugo.

As you model each sentence, ask the student to listen to *where* or *when*.

DRILL: Combining Sentences

Teacher gives two sentences which the student must combine using *where* or *when*.

Teacher	**Student**
The farm was 200 miles from the city. Carlos lived there. The farm was 200 miles from the city where Carlos lived.	The farm was 200 miles from the city where Carlos lived.
Monday is the day. I will see Jason then. Monday is the day when I will see Jason.	Monday is the day when I will see Jason.

Carlos went to the farm.
Maria was picking corn there.

This is the city.
I was born here.

This is the bank.
I keep my money here.

Monday is the day.
I will see Jason then.

7:30 is the time.
The plane will arrive then.

Tomorrow is the day.
I start my English classes then.

© New Readers Press. All rights reserved.

ORAL EVALUATION

1. Review the adjective opposites by doing the drill on Answering Questions. Student should know all of the adjectives.
2. Review *no* and *not* by doing the Transformation Drill.
3. Review *so that* by doing the drill on Combining Sentences.
4. Review adjective clauses with *where* and *when* by doing the drill on Combining Sentences.

II. Reading and Writing

BOOK 3: Lesson 23-B

Complete Lesson 23-B in book 3, following the instructions given in *Laubach Way to Reading Teacher's Edition 3*. Adapt the wording of the suggested teacher's instructions to the student as needed for your ESL student's comprehension.

ADDITIONAL WRITTEN PRACTICE

After completing Lesson 23-B in book 3, have the student do the practices for Lesson 23 in workbook 3.

© New Readers Press. All rights reserved.

Lesson 24-A

OBJECTIVES

When a student completes this lesson, he should be able to:

1. Say vocabulary about the handicapped.
2. Use the words *wild* and *tame*.
3. Use the word *nearly*.
4. Say the vocabulary about Braille.
5. Use the verb *trust*.
6. Use the verbs of the senses: *see, hear, smell, feel, taste*.
7. Use *able* + infinitive, as in *She is able to see*.

VISUAL AIDS

None.

I. Conversation Skills

VOCABULARY: The Handicapped

A blind person cannot see.
A deaf person cannot hear.
These people are handicapped. They have handicaps.
There are other kinds of handicaps.
Some people get a handicap after a sickness.

DRILL: Question and Answer Drill

Teacher asks questions to elicit the vocabulary items.

Teacher	**Student**
Who cannot see? A blind person cannot see.	A blind person cannot see.
Who cannot hear? A deaf person cannot hear.	A deaf person cannot hear.

When do some people become handicapped?
What handicaps do some people have?
Who cannot see?
Who cannot hear?

© New Readers Press. All rights reserved.

VOCABULARY: *wild* and *tame*

Some animals in the woods are wild.
Dogs and cats are tame.

VOCABULARY: The Use of *nearly*

Anne Sullivan was nearly blind when she was a girl.
It's nearly 7:30 p.m.

As you model each sentence, ask the student to listen to *nearly*.
Explain that *nearly* means the same as *almost*.

DRILL: Expansion Drill

Teacher gives a sentence which the student repeats, adding *nearly*.

Teacher	**Student**
It's 7:30.	
It's nearly 7:30.	It's nearly 7:30.
I am 35.	
I am nearly 35.	I am nearly 35.

I'm ready.
It's time to stop.
It's October.
It's 10 o'clock.
The movie is over.
Anne Sullivan was blind when she was a girl.

VOCABULARY: *Braille*

Blind people learn how to read Braille.
Braille is a way of writing with raised dots.
Blind people touch the raised dots with their fingers.

© New Readers Press. All rights reserved.

VOCABULARY: The Verb *trust*

Helen Keller believed in Anne Sullivan.
Helen was not afraid.
She trusted Anne.

VOCABULARY: Verbs of the Senses

We see with our eyes.
We hear with our ears.
We smell with our noses.
We feel with our hands.
We taste with our tongues.

As you model each sentence, act out the meaning of the verb.

VOCABULARY: Past Tense of Verbs of the Senses

We saw his car yesterday.
We heard the music last night.
We smelled the cake in the oven.
We felt the Braille.
We tasted the cake.

DRILL: Transformation Drill

Teacher gives a statement in the present tense which the student transforms into the past tense.

Teacher	Student
I see his car now. I saw his car yesterday.	I saw his car yesterday.
We hear the music. We heard the music.	We heard the music.
We smell the bread. Helen feels the Braille. We taste the bread. She sees the boy. I hear something in the kitchen.	

© New Readers Press. All rights reserved.

STRUCTURE FOCUS: *be* + *able* + Infinitive

I can hear you very well.
I am able to hear you very well.

I can't see the blackboard.
I am not able to see the blackboard.

Can you see the blackboard?
Are you able to see the blackboard?

---

1. Teacher models each pair of sentences, asking the student to listen to *able to*. Student listens. Explain that *able to* means *can*.
2. Teacher models each pair of sentences. Student repeats only the sentence with *able to*.

Note: *Able* means "having the ability" to do something. *Can* often expresses the same meaning, but it may also be used to express the meaning of "having the right" or "having the permission" to do something, as in *Can we park here?*

DRILL: Transformation Drill

Teacher gives a sentence with *can* which the student changes into a sentence with *able to*.

Teacher	**Student**
I can't come to the party. I'm not able to come to the party.	I'm not able to come to the party.
Can he walk without help? Is he able to walk without help?	Is he able to walk without help?
Can she fly an airplane?	
A cat can see in the dark.	
I can't answer that question.	
Can he run fast?	
He can't work full time.	
Can you see the blackboard?	
I can't see the blackboard.	
I can hear you very well.	

© New Readers Press. All rights reserved.

STRUCTURE FOCUS: Past Tense with *able*

Carla was able to finish her homework quickly last night.
Joe Stone was able to quit smoking in a few months.

Mr. and Mrs. Hunt were not able to go to sleep.
Helen Keller was not able to hear or speak.

As you model each sentence, ask the student to listen to *was able to* or *were able to.*

DRILL: Expansion Drill

Teacher gives words which the student uses in a negative past tense statement with *I was not able to.*

Teacher	**Student**
go to sleep I was not able to go to sleep.	I was not able to go to sleep.
lift that heavy box I was not able to lift that heavy box.	I was not able to lift that heavy box.

finish my homework
go to the concert
hear what she was saying
save any money
find a cheap car
wait for you
go to sleep
lift that heavy box

© New Readers Press. All rights reserved.

STRUCTURE FOCUS: Future Tense with *able*

I will be able to help you tomorrow.
Carlos will not be able to save any money next month.
Will you be able to finish your work by five o'clock?

As you model each sentence, ask the student to listen to *will be able to.*

DRILL: Making Sentences

Teacher gives a *when* clause and a phrase. Student uses these in a sentence with *will be able to* in the main clause.

Teacher	**Student**
When Carlos gets a better job... buy a car When Carlos gets a better job, he will be able to buy a car.	When Carlos gets a better job, he will be able to buy a car.
When it snows... go skiing When it snows, we will be able to go skiing.	When it snows, we will be able to go skiing.

When spring comes...
play baseball

When I finish doing the dishes...
help you with your homework

When Jill is 16...
get a driver's license

When the weekend comes...
sleep later

When Carlos gets a better job...
buy a car

When it snows...
go skiing

© New Readers Press. All rights reserved.

ORAL EVALUATION

1. Review vocabulary about the handicapped by doing the Question and Answer Drill. Student should know all the items.
2. Review the use of *nearly* by doing the Expansion Drill.
3. Review the past tense of verbs of the senses by doing the Transformation Drill.
4. Review *be* + *able* + infinitive by doing the Transformation Drill.
5. Review the past tense with *able* by doing the Expansion Drill.
6. Review the future tense with *able* by doing the drill on Making Sentences.

II. Reading and Writing

BOOK 3: Lesson 24-A

Complete Lesson 24-A in book 3, following the instructions given in *Laubach Way to Reading Teacher's Edition 3*. Adapt the wording of the suggested teacher's instructions to the student as needed for your ESL student's comprehension.

Note: In workbook 3, all of the exercises for Lesson 24 should be done following Lesson 24-B.

© New Readers Press. All rights reserved.

Lesson 24-B

OBJECTIVES

When a student completes this lesson, he should be able to:

1. Say some adjectives and related abstract nouns, such as *free* and *freedom.*
2. Say some words about civil rights.
3. Say some words about protests.
4. Use the word *boycott.*
5. Say some words about the Nobel Peace Prize.
6. Say the names of some cities in Alabama and its state capital, and recognize Washington, D.C., as the capital of the United States.

VISUAL AIDS

1. *LWE Illustrations 3*, pp. 55–56.
2. *Changes*, p. 27.

I. Conversation Skills

VOCABULARY: Adjectives and Abstract Nouns

---

1. There is beauty in the sky and trees.
   These things are beautiful.

2. Martin Luther King had courage.
   He was not afraid. He was brave.
   He wanted justice for his people.
   He wanted all people to be fair to his people.

3. Martin Luther King did not want violence.
   He did not want people to be hurt.
   He did not want people to be violent.

4. Martin Luther King wanted equality for his people.
   He wanted his people to be the same as all other people.
   He wanted everyone to be equal.

5. Martin Luther King wanted freedom for his people.
   He wanted all people to be free and have their rights.

---

1. Teacher models the sentences in groups, as numbered. Student listens.
2. Teacher models the sentences. Student repeats after each sentence.

© New Readers Press. All rights reserved.

VOCABULARY: Civil Rights

People have the right to say what they want.
People have the right to go to any church they want.
People have the right to go to any meetings they want.
These are some of the civil rights that people in the United States have.
The United States cannot make a law to take away these civil rights.

1. Teacher says each sentence, asking the student to listen to *right* or *civil rights*. Student listens.
2. Teacher models the sentences. Student repeats after each sentence.
3. Teacher asks the student to tell some of the civil rights that people in the United States have.

VOCABULARY: Protests

When people's civil rights are taken away, they protest.
When people protest, they march together.
These people are protesters.
People who walk together to protest are marchers.

Martin Luther King was a leader.
He led protesters in a march.
He was put in jail.
He was arrested by the police and put in jail.

Use the pictures on pp. 27 and 28 of *Changes* that show Dr. King leading a protest and in jail to help the student understand this vocabulary.

DRILL: Answering Questions

Using the pictures in *Changes*, ask the student questions to elicit the vocabulary about protests, such as:

Where is Dr. King? (in jail)
What is Martin Luther King doing in this picture? (leading a march)
Who are the people in the picture? (protesters)
What are the people in the picture doing? (protesting)

VOCABULARY: *boycott*

The black ministers planned a bus boycott.
They asked people to stop riding the city buses.

Explain that a boycott is a way of protesting. In a boycott, people stop buying or using something.

© New Readers Press. All rights reserved.

VOCABULARY: *The Nobel Prize*

Martin Luther King was a good leader.
He won a big prize.
He won the Nobel Peace Prize for leading
the non-violent protests for civil rights.

As you model the sentences, ask the student to listen to the words *Nobel Peace Prize*. Use the photo of this on p. 55 of *LWE Illustrations 3*.

VOCABULARY: Cities and Capitals

Alabama is a state in the South.
Selma and Birmingham are cities in Alabama.
Montgomery is another city in Alabama.
Montgomery is the capital of Alabama. It is the state capital.

Washington, D.C., is a city in the East.
It is the capital of the United States.

Use the United States map on p. 53 of *LWE Illustrations 3* to locate Alabama in the South and to show Washington, D.C. Use the map of Alabama on p. 56 to show the cities in Alabama.

Note: You may also want to teach the capital of your state and mark it on the map on p. 53.

DRILL: Answering Questions

Using the two maps, ask questions which elicit the vocabulary items, such as:

Where is Montgomery?
What is the capital of Alabama?
Where is Alabama?
What is Washington, D.C.?
Where is Selma?
What are three cities in Alabama?
Is Alabama a city or a state?
Is Washington, D.C. a city or a state?
Where is Birmingham?

© New Readers Press. All rights reserved.

ORAL EVALUATION

Review the new vocabulary as needed by having the student repeat the sentences or by using the drills provided.

II. Reading and Writing

BOOK 3: Lesson 24-B

Complete Lesson 24-B in book 3, following the instructions given in *Laubach Way to Reading Teacher's Edition 3*. Adapt the wording of the suggested teacher's instructions to the student as needed for your ESL student's comprehension.

ADDITIONAL WRITTEN PRACTICE

After completing Lesson 24-B in book 3, have the student do the practices for Lesson 24 in workbook 3.

© New Readers Press. All rights reserved.

Oral Evaluation for Book 3

This Oral Evaluation covers the material introduced in the Conversation Skills. It is divided into two parts. Part I is a review of 75 vocabulary items, grouped according to topic. Part II is a review of the basic structural patterns taught, grouped according to patterns.

PART I. VOCABULARY

Procedure: The 75 vocabulary items in this part appear in the Teacher's Evaluation Form which follows. To conduct this part of the Oral Evaluation, follow the directions below for each set of items.

Items 1–4: Use p. 4 of *LWE Illustrations 3*. Elicit the names of the food items pictured. You may begin by saying: "When Mrs. Falco goes to the supermarket to buy food, what does she buy?"

Items 5–9: Use pp. 5–6 of *LWE Illustrations 3*. Have the student identify vegetables. You may ask: "What's this?" or "What are these?"

Items 10–14: Use pp. 10–13 of *LWE Illustrations 3*. Elicit *play* or *go* plus the activity being pictured. You may ask: "What are they doing?"

Items 15–20: Use pp. 14–15 of *LWE Illustrations 3*. Ask the student to identify some basic tools and equipment. You may ask: "What's this?"

Items 21–25: Use p. 16 of *LWE Illustrations 3*. Ask the student to identify parts of the face. You may say: "Carla has a pretty face," and then ask, "What is this?" or "What are these?"

Items 26–27: Use p. 20 of *LWE Illustrations 3*. Elicit the activity picture. You may ask: "What is this person doing?"

Items 28–34: Use pp. 21–23 of *LWE Illustrations 3*. Ask the student to name some items of personal grooming. You may ask: "What do you wash your face with?" and so on, pointing to the items as necessary.

Items 35–38: Student should respond with an appropriate adjective as you ask:

35. How do we feel when a friend yells at us?
36. How do we feel when a friend gets sick?
37. How do we feel when a friend gets better?
38. How does Mrs. Green feel when her son comes home late?

Items 39–43: The student should give the adjective opposite to the one you use. To begin, say: "I say the book is big. You say the opposite—the book is small." Then use the cues below.

39. Beans are cheap. Meat is _____.
40. The day is bright. The night is _____.
41. The big building is high. The small building is _____.
42. His hands are dirty. My hands are _____.
43. This book is open. That one is _____.

© New Readers Press. All rights reserved.

Items 44–48: Use p. 27 of *LWE Illustrations 3*. Elicit the prepositions. You may ask: "Where is Ray sitting?" and so on.

Items 49–53: Use pp. 30–31 of *LWE Illustrations 3*. Elicit names of items used for cleaning. You may say: "When Steve cleans the shop, he uses many things. What are these things?" Then, point to each item.

Items 54–58: Elicit verbs about feelings. You may ask the questions below. You may also need to act out the verbs.

54. What does Fran do when something is funny?
55. What does Fran do when she is happy?
56. What does Fran do when she is not happy?
57. What does Fran do when she is very sad?
58. What does Fran do when she is angry?

Items 59–61: Elicit the irregular plurals. You may say: "I have one knife; you have two _____," and so on.

Items 62–64: Use pp. 40–41 of *LWE Illustrations 3*. Elicit names of public employees. You may ask: "Who is this?"

Items 65–68: Elicit the names of the seasons. You may ask:

65. What season is very hot? People go swimming then.
66. In what season do the leaves of the trees get red and yellow?
67. In what season do the trees get green?
68. What season is very cold?

Items 69–72: Elicit names of schools. You may ask:

69. Where do young children go to school first?
70. Where do they go after kindergarten?
71–72. Where do teenagers go to school?

Items 73–75: You may ask:

73. What do you call the people of a country?
74. What do you call people who move into a new country to live?
75. What do you call people who leave their country because they are afraid?

Scoring: Assess your student's performance and check the appropriate column on the Teacher's Evaluation Form.

— Check column 1 if the student identifies the item fairly quickly and with fairly understandable pronunciation.

— Check column 2 if the student identifies the item with some hesitation but with fairly understandable pronunciation.

— Check column 3 if the student identifies the picture incorrectly, or if, after a short wait, he cannot identify it at all.

No matter how the student answers, do not tell him he is right or wrong. Do not look disappointed or disapproving if he gives you an incorrect answer or does not answer at all. Go on briskly with the evaluation.

© New Readers Press. All rights reserved.

PART I. VOCABULARY: Teacher's Evaluation Form

Student's name ______________________________ Date ____________________

1. ham	1	2	3
2. hamburger			
3. beans			
4. tea			
5. tomatoes			
6. lettuce			
7. carrots			
8. potatoes			
9. onions			
10. play cards			
11. play football			
12. play hockey			
13. go swimming			
14. go skiing			
15. hammer			
16. screwdriver			
17. saw			
18. scissors			
19. ladder			
20. pail			
21. hair			
22. lips			
23. cheeks			
24. teeth			
25. ears			
26. take a bath			
27. take a shower			
28. soap			
29. towel			
30. washcloth			
31. toothbrush			
32. razor			
33. shampoo			
34. comb			
35. angry			
36. sad			
37. glad			
38. upset			

39. expensive	1	2	3
40. dark			
41. low			
42. clean			
43. shut			
44. between			
45. next to			
46. in back of			
47. in front of			
48. in the back of			
49. broom			
50. dustpan			
51. mop			
52. vacuum cleaner			
53. sponge			
54. laugh			
55. smile			
56. frown			
57. cry			
58. shout			
59. knives			
60. feet			
61. children			
62. police officer			
63. firefighter			
64. mail carrier			
65. summer			
66. fall			
67. spring			
68. winter			
69. kindergarten			
70. elementary school			
71. junior high school			
72. high school			
73. citizens			
74. immigrants			
75. refugees			
Part I Totals			

This page may be photocopied for classroom use only. All other rights reserved. © New Readers Press

Procedure: In this part, the student is asked to produce the major structural patterns that have been taught. The 75 items in this part are listed below. They are grouped in sets according to structural patterns.

In each set of items, there are two examples for you to use to show the student what is expected of him. Say both the teacher's cue and the expected student response. Have the student repeat the response after you.

For the remaining (numbered) items in the set, give only the cues. Do not prompt the student or help him. If he seems confused, simply repeat the two examples given, having him repeat the responses after you. If he cannot do one set, proceed briskly to the next one without showing signs of disapproval or discouragement.

SET A: Past Tense with Irregular Verbs

Teacher's cue	Student response
What did you send your mother?	I sent her a letter.
When did Ed cut the grass?	He cut it yesterday.

1. What did David lend Tom?
2. Who cut the bread?
3. How much did Jason spend?
4. Where did Ed sleep?
5. What did Carla give the baby?
6. Who did Mr. Chan speak to?
7. Who did Mr. Chan shake hands with?
8. When did Kim break the dish?
9. What did the man steal?
10. What color coat did Gail choose?

SET B: Questions in the Present Perfect Tense

Teacher's cue	Student response
She painted a house.	Has she ever painted a house?
She washed the dog.	Has she ever washed the dog?

11. He slept on the floor.
12. Ed spent a lot of money.
13. She sang the song.
14. Carla gave him some money.
15. Jason ate all the cake.
16. David swept the kitchen.
17. Gail kept the money.
18. Mr. Oliver lived in New York City.
19. Fran ran in the race.
20. Mr. Chan shook the teacher's hand.

© New Readers Press. All rights reserved.

SET C: Statements in the Passive Voice

Teacher's cue	Student response
Someone steals the ring.	The ring is stolen.
Someone broke the lock.	The lock was broken.

21. Someone wrote this book.
22. Someone steals the book.
23. Someone drove the truck.
24. People speak English in many countries.
25. People read the book in English.

SET D: Reflexive Pronouns

Teacher's cue	Student response
Who stopped the washing machine?	It stopped itself.
Who are we buying the books for?	We are buying them for ourselves.

26. Who hurt the cat?
27. Who was I talking to?
28. Who is David buying the shirt for?
29. Who are they getting the books for?
30. Who is Carla baking the cake for?

SET E: Verbs + Gerunds or Infinitives

Teacher's cue	Student response
I'll learn	I'll learn to read.
I've finished	I've finished working.

31. She'll plan
32. He has quit
33. I'll tell her
34. Jason stopped
35. He wants
36. He has practiced
37. It takes 30 minutes
38. I'm tired of
39. Lee is worried about
40. It's time

SET F: Sequence of Tenses in Clauses

Teacher's cue	Student response
We'll see if	We'll see if Ellen can help us.
I could speak Italian when	I could speak Italian when I was a child.

41. When Carla calls
42. I can't tell if
43. When the telephone rings
44. I'll ask Ann if
45. When the teacher talked

© New Readers Press. All rights reserved.

SET G: Short Answers to Questions

Teacher's cue	Student response
Is Ann in class?	No, she isn't.
Did Fran go running yesterday?	Yes, she did.

46. Could she help you?
47. Will you drive me home, please?
48. Has Fran been running for a year?
49. Can Jason fix the stairs?
50. Should Tom smoke so much?
51. Are you able to see the blackboard?
52. Would you mind closing the window?

SET H: Short Answers to Questions

Teacher's cue	Student response
Fran and Mike are retired	Fran and Mike are retired, aren't they?
You had better wear a heavy coat	You had better wear a heavy coat, hadn't you?

53. You wouldn't mind helping me
54. People don't go fishing in the river
55. You can't see the church from here
56. Mr. Chan has met his teacher
57. Carla can speak English
58. The police didn't find the ring
59. Tom hasn't ever played soccer
60. They will play hockey in Canada

SET I: Adjective Clauses with *that*

Teacher's cue	Student response
I like the frame. Gail put the picture in it.	I like the frame that Gail put the picture in.
Lee went to see the tree. He hit the tree.	Lee went to see the tree that he hit.

61. You can keep the money. Mrs. Green gave you the money.
62. They painted the apartment. They lived in the apartment.
63. Ann goes to a class. The class meets in a church.
64. Ray and Kay are going to a movie. The movie is about a little girl.
65. He can read the book. I gave him the book.

© New Readers Press. All rights reserved.

SET J: Statements with *but ... anyway*

Teacher's cue	**Student response**
There was ice on the road.	
He drove fast.	There was ice on the road, but he drove fast anyway.
Steve tore his shirt.	
He wore it.	Steve tore his shirt, but he wore it anyway.

66. It was raining. They went camping.
67. This dress is old. I'm going to wear it.
68. It's late. I'm going to call Joan.

SET K: Statements with *as ... as*

Teacher's cue	**Student response**
Pete is sad. Lee is sad.	Pete is as sad as Lee.
Fran ran fast. Kim ran fast.	Fran ran as fast as Kim.

69. Lee Chan speaks slowly. I speak slowly.
70. Jane's hair is dark. Gail's hair is dark.
71. Mrs. Green is worried. Lee is worried.

SET L: Verbs with Prepositions

Teacher's cue	**Student response**
Ed—afraid—dogs	Ed is afraid of dogs.
Mrs. Green—angry—Lee	Mrs. Green is angry at Lee.

72. Pete—worried—mother
73. Carla—right—the price of the book
74. We—tired—television
75. I—interested—this book

Scoring: Assess your student's performance and check the appropriate column on the Teacher's Evaluation Form that follows. Evaluate the student's performance on a scale of 1 to 3, using the same criteria as for the vocabulary:

— Check column 1 if the student gives the correct structure, responding fairly quickly and with fairly understandable pronunciation.

— Check column 2 if the student gives the correct structure with some hesitation but with fairly understandable pronunciation.

— Check column 3 if the student cannot form the structure correctly or if, after a short wait, he cannot respond at all.

Evaluate only the structure in question. For example, suppose the student is asked to change a statement into a question in the present perfect tense. After the cue "Mr. Oliver lived in New York City," he says: "Has Mr. Oliver ever lived in New York?" responding fairly quickly and with good pronunciation. In such a case, check column 1 even though the student has omitted the word *City*. He *has* formed the question correctly in the present perfect tense, and that is the structure in question.

© New Readers Press. All rights reserved.

PART II. STRUCTURAL PATTERNS: Teacher's Evaluation Form

Student name ______________________________ Date ____________________

		1	2	3
Set A	1.	____	____	____
	2.	____	____	____
	3.	____	____	____
	4.	____	____	____
	5.	____	____	____
	6.	____	____	____
	7.	____	____	____
	8.	____	____	____
	9.	____	____	____
	10.	____	____	____
Set B	11.	____	____	____
	12.	____	____	____
	13.	____	____	____
	14.	____	____	____
	15.	____	____	____
	16.	____	____	____
	17.	____	____	____
	18.	____	____	____
	19.	____	____	____
	20.	____	____	____
Set C	21.	____	____	____
	22.	____	____	____
	23.	____	____	____
	24.	____	____	____
	25.	____	____	____
Set D	26.	____	____	____
	27.	____	____	____
	28.	____	____	____
	29.	____	____	____
	30.	____	____	____
Set E	31.	____	____	____
	32.	____	____	____
	33.	____	____	____
	34.	____	____	____
	35.	____	____	____
	36.	____	____	____
	37.	____	____	____
	38.	____	____	____
	39.	____	____	____
	40.	____	____	____
Set F	41.	____	____	____
	42.	____	____	____
	43.	____	____	____
	44.	____	____	____
	45.	____	____	____
Set G	46.	____	____	____
	47.	____	____	____
	48.	____	____	____
	49.	____	____	____
	50.	____	____	____
	51.	____	____	____
	52.	____	____	____
Set H	53.	____	____	____
	54.	____	____	____
	55.	____	____	____
	56.	____	____	____
	57.	____	____	____
	58.	____	____	____
	59.	____	____	____
	60.	____	____	____
Set I	61.	____	____	____
	62.	____	____	____
	63.	____	____	____
	64.	____	____	____
	65.	____	____	____
Set J	66.	____	____	____
	67.	____	____	____
	68.	____	____	____
Set K	69.	____	____	____
	70.	____	____	____
	71.	____	____	____
Set L	72.	____	____	____
	73.	____	____	____
	74.	____	____	____
	75.	____	____	____
Part II Totals		____	____	____

This page may be photocopied for classroom use only. All other rights reserved. © New Readers Press

EVALUATING THE STUDENT'S PERFORMANCE

Part I. Vocabulary

If your student gets a total of 60 or more checks in columns 1 and 2, he is ready to begin book 4.

You should, however, look over the vocabulary items he missed and review them, a few at a time, in subsequent lessons.

If your student gets a total of 45–59 checks in columns 1 and 2, you must spend some time reviewing the vocabulary items he missed before beginning book 4.

Anything less than 44 checks in columns 1 and 2 indicates need for extensive review before beginning book 4.

Always combine review of vocabulary with review of structural patterns. For example, if the student was unable to name any of the tools, combine a review of those items with a review of question and answer patterns.

Part II. Structural Patterns

If your student gets a total of 60 or more checks in columns 1 and 2, he is ready to begin book 4.

It is important, however, that you analyze the items he missed. If he missed most or all of the items in a section, be sure to review that structural pattern again before beginning book 4.

If your student gets less than 60 in columns 1 and 2, it is especially important to review any basic structures he is having difficulty with before beginning book 4.

Review only those structures that caused the most difficulty. If a student missed only one item in a section, review would generally not be necessary. Watch for sections in which the student missed most or all of the items, and review those structures in particular. In general, the more checks in column 3 in a particular section, the more time you will need to spend reviewing that structure.

© New Readers Press. All rights reserved.

Word List for Conversation Skills

Words that appear in the list below are items introduced in the Vocabulary and Structure Focus sections of this guide. Items are listed only when the student himself is asked to produce them. Items that occur only in the Dialogs are not listed. The numbers refer to lesson numbers, not pages.

The main entries are the normal dictionary-entry forms, including irregular verb forms. Examples of usage and structures are listed under the main entries. A dash indicates that the main-entry word is taught only in the expression given below it. Variants formed by adding endings to root words are not listed.

Listings in boldface refer to categories of words that are introduced as a group. (The boldface words themselves are not part of the student's vocabulary, however, unless they are listed elsewhere.)

Lesson	Main Entries, with Variants and Structures
24–A	able
19	above
9	account
10	adult
20	afford
14	afraid
1	after
7	again
19	against
11	age
23-A	agree
19	ahead
7	air
24-B	Alabama
15	almost
5	already
21	although
13	a.m.
22	Americans
7	angry
1	animals
5	any more
8	anyone
8	anything
—	anyway
21	but ... anyway
11	application
10	appointment
24-B	arrest
14	arrive
14	as ... as
21	as far as
2	babysits
2	babysitter
7	back
8	in back of
8	in the back of
19	back and forth
15	back up
5	bake
10	Baker (family name)
8	banana
22	band (music)
9	bank
18	bank (of the river)
3	baseball
3	basketball
18	beach
1	beans
24-B	beautiful
24-B	beauty
21	became
14	because
21	become
17	**Bedding**
1	beef
12	been
1	before
19	behind
19	below
8	best
15	better
19	had better
22	beverages
7	**Beverages**
1	bill
24-B	Birmingham
11	birth
11	birthday
17	blanket
19	blew
24-A	blind
20	blouse
19	blow
18	blow one's nose
19	blown
18	boil (v.)
11	born
16	both
24-B	boycott
24-A	Braille
24-B	brave
16	break
10	take a break
7	bright
16	bring
16	broke
16	broken
9	broom
4	brush
21	but ... anyway
5	cake
22	California
3	call
21	came
5	camera
18	can opener
10	Canada
22	Canadians
24-B	capital
3	cards
1	Carla

© New Readers Press. All rights reserved.

Lesson	Main Entries, with Variants and Structures
23-B	Carlos
2	carrots
18	catch cold
13	cemetery
20	cheapest
3	check
4	cheeks
1	chicken
16	choose
16	chose
16	chosen
22	citizens
24-B	civil rights
7	clean
21	clean up
9	cleaner
2	clerk
4	climb
18	coffee pot
18	cold (have a cold)
21	college
6	comb
21	come (past participle)
18	cook
18	**Cooking Appliances**
1	cost
23-B	cotton
16	could
16	couldn't
10	countries
24-B	courage
1	cow
24-A	crippled
23-B	crops
18	Cuba
22	Cubans
2	cup
1	cut (past tense)
10	Dallas
—	date
11	date of birth
10	make a date
1	David
13	day
24-A	deaf
14	depart
20	department
22	dessert
13	die
20	directory
9	dirt
7	dirty
23-A	disagree
24-A	dots
21	drink up
16	driven
7	driver
16	drove
12	drugstore
22	drums
5	drunk (past participle)
9	dustpan
8	each
20	each other
4	ears
22	east
3	easy
21	eat up
5	eaten
9	eighteenth
9	eighth
9	eightieth
21	elementary school
9	eleventh
13	Ellen
18	end of
24-B	equal
24-B	equality
20	every other
8	everyone
8	everything
5	expensive
4	eyes
4	face
24-B	fair (adj.)
1	Falco (family name)
18	fall
15	farther
23-B	**Farm Workers**
12	feet
7	felt
11	female
9	fifteenth
9	fifth
9	fiftieth
5	film
15	fine (a fine man)
5	finish
21	finish up
16	firefighter
13	flight
13	flight attendant
22	Florida
13	fly (v.)
19	follow
1	food
1	**Food Items**
12	foot (measurement)
3	football
5	forgave
21	forget
5	forgive
5	forgiven
21	forgot
21	forgotten
9	fortieth
15	forward
9	fourteenth
9	fourth
5	frame
23-A	free
24-B	freedom
16	freeze
23-B	friendly
7	front
8	in front of
8	in the front of
12	frown
16	froze
16	frozen
8	fruit
18	fry
18	frying pan
2	full-time
13	funeral
22	future
4	Gail
22	Garcia (family name)
14	gate (at airport)
4	get
5	given

© New Readers Press. All rights reserved.

Lesson	Main Entries, with Variants and Structures
7	glad
5	got
21	gotten
8	grape
13	grave
22	guitar
19	had better
4	hair
6	hairbrush
6	hairdryer
2	half
1	ham
1	hamburger
4	hammer
24-A	handicap
24-A	handicapped
3	hard (difficult)
23-B	hard-working
5	hasn't
5	haven't
3	have to
2	head (of lettuce)
5	herself
4	high
21	high school
5	himself
3	hockey
17	hope
13	hour
22	Hugo
9	hundredth
7	ice
7	iced
11	if
22	immigrants
12	inch
10	infant
21	instead
14	interested
4	invite
18	island
2	it (impersonal)
5	itself
5	I've
24-B	jail
5	Jane
1	Jason
18	Joan
17	Joe
22	join
21	junior high
24-B	justice
2	Kay
15	leaves (n. pl.)
24-B	led
6	Lee
8	lemon
1	lend
1	lent
15	less
1	lettuce
11	license
11	license plate
4	lips
—	little (amount)
15	I have little money.
18	load (v.)
15	loaves
22	look forward to
1	Lopez (family name)
7	low
23-B	lovely
16	mail carriers
11	male
18	map
24-B	march
24-B	marcher
3	Mason (family name)
17	mattress
5	may (for permission)
7	mean
7	meant
12	**Measures, Length**
2	**Measures, Liquid**
1	meat
10	medicine
22	member
22	menu
10	mess
22	Mexicans
22	Mexico
18	middle
23-B	migrant
12	Mike
12	mile
—	mind
18	Would you mind...?
13	minister
22	Minnesota
13	minute
10	mistake
24-B	Montgomery
9	mop
10	more
20	most
1	music
11	must
5	myself
4	nails
24-A	nearly
8	next to
3	nice
17	nightgown
9	nineteenth
9	ninetieth
9	ninth
23-B	no (modifier)
8	no one
24-B	Nobel Peace Prize
22	north
22	North America
8	nothing
9	**Numbers, Ordinal**
18	Oak (family name)
18	ocean
16	Oh
16	Oh, no!
16	Oh, well
2	onions
7	open (adj.)
8	orange
5	ourselves
4	order (v.)
20	out of order
20	in order
7	outdoors
18	oven
3	paid
4	pail
4	paint
17	pajamas

© New Readers Press. All rights reserved.

Lesson	Main Entries, with Variants and Structures
2	part-time
9	parts
4	**Parts of the Face**
7	passenger
22	past (time expression)
2	pat (of butter)
3	payday
24-B	peace
8	peach
8	pear
2	peas
6	**Personal Grooming**
9	Pete
22	piano
22	pie
1	Pig
17	pillow
13	pilot
—	pity
13	What a pity!
4	places
5	plate
3	play (v.)
4	pliers
13	p.m.
16	police officer
1	pork
20	Porter (family name)
2	potato
2	pound of
13	pray
22	present (time expression)
1	price
12	print (v.)
24-B	prize
24-B	protest
24-B	protester
18	pull
18	push
1	put (past tense)
2	**Quantities, Food in**
2	quarter (of a cup)
5	quit
12	race
24-A	raised
2	Ray
6	razor
22	refugees
4	remember
3	rent
9	repair
18	rest (v.)
22	restaurant
12	retired
2	rice
16	ridden
11	ride (v.)
24-B	rights
18	road
18	roast
17	robe
16	rode
16	Romano (family name)
2	Rosa
17	Rose
5	rung (v.)
7	sad
1	salad
—	sale
12	for sale
9	sales tax
12	salesperson
18	sand
18	sandy
5	sang
16	sanitation worker
9	save
9	savings account
4	saw (n.)
21	school
4	scissors
4	screwdriver
4	screws
18	seasons
7	seat
9	second (2nd)
13	seconds (in a minute)
24-B	Selma
1	sent
13	services
9	seventeenth
9	seventh
9	seventieth
11	sex
17	shaken
4	shall
—	shame
13	That's a shame!
6	shampoo
23-A	share
17	sheets
15	shelf
15	shelves
17	shook
18	shore (n.)
14	should
14	shouldn't
12	shout
6	shower
7	shut (adj.)
1	shut (past tense)
24-A	sickness
12	sign (v.)
16	silver
1	singer
9	sixteenth
9	sixth
9	sixtieth
3	skiing
3	skating
7	sky
17	sleepwear
20	sleeves
7	slept
17	slippers
24-A	smell
18	sneeze
16	so
19	so ... that
6	soap
8	someone
8	something
1	song
18	sore throat
22	south
19	speed limit
1	spend
18	spend time
1	spent
17	spoke
17	spoken

© New Readers Press. All rights reserved.

Lesson	Main Entries, with Variants and Structures
9	sponge
20	sportshirt
18	spring
10	state (n.)
16	steal
7	steering wheel
9	Steve
2	stick (of butter)
5	still
16	stole
16	stolen
24-A	Sullivan, Anne
18	summer
5	sung
20	swear
7	sweep
7	swept
20	swore
20	sworn
17	taken
24-A	tame
24-A	taste
1	tea
18	teapot
10	teenager
4	teeth
9	tenth
11	test
11	tester
10	Texas
10	than
9	that
5	themselves
13	"There, there"
9	third
9	thirteenth
9	thirtieth
19	threw
18	throat
19	throw
19	thrown
13	ticket
12	tie (in a race)
—	time
13	it takes time to
13	it's time for
13	it's time to
14	timetable
14	tired of
18	toast
18	toaster
1	tomato
16	Tony
17	took
4	**Tools and Equipment**
6	toothbrush
6	toothpaste
20	torn
24-A	touch
6	towel
23-B	train (v.)
9	trash can
7	trees
24-A	trust
15	turns
9	twelfth
9	twentieth
3	twice
23-B	unfriendly
22	union (labor)
10	United States
21	university
21	until
7	upset
9	vacuum (v.)
9	vacuum cleaner
2	vegetables
24-B	violence
24-B	violent
4	wait
22	wait for
22	wait on
17	wake
17	waked
6	washcloth
24-B	Washington, D.C.
8	watermelon
18	way
5	wedding
22	west
4	when
12	while
13	why
24-A	wild
12	win
7	wine
12	winner
18	winter
15	wives
17	woke
15	woman
15	women
23-A	wonder
4	wood
20	worn
14	worried
15	worse
8	worst
18	Would you mind...?
11	written
17	wrote
12	yard (measurement)
5	yet
5	yourself
5	yourselves
19	zero
11	zip code number

© New Readers Press. All rights reserved.

Word List for Level 3

Book 3 and its correlated reader *Changes* introduce the 543 words and 3 symbols listed below. Variants with *-s, -es, -'s, -s'*, *-ed, -ing,* and *-er* (comparative) are not listed except when *y* is changed to *i* before an ending. New words are listed in their root form when they are used with these previously taught endings. Variants are indented under their root word. Italics indicate a variant of a known word or a word taught earlier as a sight word which is reintroduced and taught phonetically at this level.

Words introduced in titles and directions are starred. The number indicates the lesson in which the word is introduced. The abbreviation *cr* stands for the correlated reader, and the number following it refers to the story number in the correlated reader.

cr. 3 able
cr. 4 act
8 ad
cr. 1 afford
7 again
11 age
15 ago
cr. 1 agree
19 ahead
13 air
cr. 3 Alabama
15 alone
13 a.m.
22 America
20 & (and)
7 angry
cr. 3 Anne
2 *answer
16 anyone
8 anything
cr. 1 anyway
2 apartment
11 application
2 April
cr. 4 arrest
14 arrive
15 as
5 ate
4 away
2 baby
cr. 1 babysit
2 babysitter
5 bake
8 baker
22 band
1 bank
7 be
8 beans
cr. 3 beauty
21 became
12 been
7 beer
20 before
cr. 3 began
15 behind
19 below
8 best
11 bicycle
22 *-biggest*
1 bill
cr. 4 Birmingham
11 birth
cr. 3 blind
18 blow
18 boat
cr. 4 bomb
cr. 1 born
16 both
cr. 4 boycott
cr. 3 Braille
12 breakfast
7 bright
21 broke
16 broken
12 bus
14 buy
13 by
5 cake
5 came
18 camp
10 Canada
cr. 1 can't
cr. 4 capital
3 card
7 care
1 Carla
cr. 2 Carlos
9 ¢ (cent)
4 chair
13 *change
7 cheap
20 -cheapest
3 check
8 cheese
14 child
14 China
5 church
17 cigarette
14 *-cities*
22 citizen
cr. 4 civil
1 class
9 clean
18 close (cloze)
18 clothes
18 coat
1 coffee
18 cold
cr. 3 college
20 corner
1 cost
cr. 2 cotton
22 country
22 -countries
cr. 3 courage
cr. 4 court
cr. 2 crop
12 cry

© New Readers Press. All rights reserved.

13	-cried	**cr. 4**	fight	**17**	home
13	-cries	**15**	find	**17**	hope
22	Cuba	**15**	fine	**22**	Hugo
22	Cuban	**15**	finish	**3**	hundred
10	Dallas	**17**	fire	**15**	husband
10	date	**14**	flight	**1**	*I*
1	David	**20**	floor	**19**	ice
3	day	**22**	Florida	**19**	icy
cr. 3	deaf	**13**	fly	**15**	ID
5	dear	**19**	follow	**cr. 3**	idea
14	depart	**21**	forget	**11**	if
17	department	**7**	forty	**1**	I'll
7	didn't	**22**	forward	**14**	I'm
13	die	**7**	fourteen	**cr. 4**	injustice
20	directory	**20**	fourth	**2**	instant
1	$ (dollar)	**5**	frame	**21**	instead
17	don't	**cr. 2**	free	**7**	it's
16	door	**cr. 4**	freedom	**cr. 4**	jail
cr. 3	dot	**22**	Friday	**5**	Jane
cr. 4	dream	**22**	future	**1**	Jason
1	drink	**4**	Gail	**cr. 1**	Jay
11	drive	**4**	gallon	**18**	Joan
11	driver	**22**	Garcia	**17**	Joe
6	dry	**14**	gate	**17**	Jones
6	-dried	**5**	gave	**cr. 4**	Jr.
8	each	**7**	glad	**cr. 4**	justice
cr. 3	ear	**1**	go	**3**	Kay
8	eat	**cr. 4**	God	**7**	keep
8	eaten	**16**	gold	**cr. 3**	Keller
7	eight	**cr. 2**	Gomez	**9**	key
7	eighteen	**cr. 4**	grave	**cr. 1**	kind
7	eighty	**12**	gray	**19**	know
7	eleven	**cr. 3**	great	**9**	labor
cr. 4	empty	**7**	Green	**2**	lady
18	end	**1**	had	**18**	lake
18	English	**14**	hair	**3**	landlady
cr. 2	enough	**1**	ham	**2**	last
cr. 4	equal	**1**	hamburger	**7**	late
cr. 4	even	**cr. 3**	handicap	**cr. 4**	lead
6	evening	**cr. 2**	handsome	**cr. 4**	leader
7	ever	**cr. 2**	hard-working	**15**	learn
12	every	**7**	*he*	**cr. 4**	led
8	everyone	**cr. 3**	hear	**13**	Lee
cr. 1	everything	**18**	heavy	**11**	license
11	eye	**cr. 3**	Helen	**15**	life
6	face	**8**	here	**14**	light
7	feel	**cr. 1**	herself	**12**	like
cr. 3	felt	**13**	high	**19**	limit
7	fifteen	**5**	*himself	**13**	line
7	fifty	**10**	hockey	**cr. 3**	lip

© New Readers Press. All rights reserved.

1	*listen*	14	night	2	*practice
18	load	7	nine	12	price
15	loaf	7	nineteen	cr. 4	prize
1	Lopez	7	ninety	cr. 4	protect
13	love	cr. 4	Nobel	cr. 4	protest
cr. 2	lovely	cr. 4	non-violent	cr. 4	protester
cr. 4	Luther	22	north	2	quart
18	made	18	nose	14	*question
6	make	18	Oak	21	quit
18	map	12	o'clock	12	race
cr. 4	march	18	October	1	radio
cr. 4	marcher	16	officer	18	rain
cr. 2	Maria	16	oh	cr. 3	raise
cr. 4	Martin	7	OK	3	Ray
cr. 2	Mary	16	old	1	*read
3	Mason	19	onto	cr. 2	read (red)
cr. 1	matter	16	open	8	reader
3	May	20	*order	22	refugee
2	me	18	over	cr. 3	remember
8	meal	cr. 3	overcome	3	rent
8	meat	cr. 2	own	9	repair
22	menu	cr. 2	Pablo	12	retired
cr. 4	met	3	paid	11	ride
22	Mexico	4	paint	5	*right
cr. 2	migrant	2	paper	18	road
12	Mike	cr. 1	parent	18	roast
12	mile	9	part	17	robe
1	milk	5	party	16	Romano
cr. 4	minister	2	pat	2	Rosa
16	*missing	3	pay	17	Rose
2	Monday	cr. 1	paycheck	14	sad
9	money	3	payday	cr. 2	sadly
cr. 4	Montgomery	cr. 4	peace	1	salad
2	month	cr. 2	peach	12	sale
6	*more	8	people	12	salesperson
22	morning	11	permit	11	same
20	most	9	Pete	19	sand
5	much	17	phone	1	sandwich
1	music	9	place	cr. 4	sat
1	*my*	5	plate	12	Saturday
6	myself	3	play	9	save
4	nail	10	player	2	*say
14	near	4	please	9	second
cr. 3	nearly	13	p.m.	5	see
7	need	16	police	cr. 4	Selma
14	never	20	Porter	1	sentence
1	next	cr. 3	possible	13	service
10	nice	2	potatoes	9	seventeen

© New Readers Press. All rights reserved.

11 sex
4 shall
cr. 1 share
20 shirt
18 shore
3 *short
19 show
cr. 3 sickness
19 side
14 sight
12 sign
cr. 4 sit-in
7 sixteen
7 sixty
14 sky
7 sleep
20 sleeve
19 slow
19 slowly
17 smell
12 smile
14 smoke
1 snack
19 snow
16 so
16 sofa
16 someone
8 something
12 sometimes
2 *sound
22 speak
19 speed
cr. 1 spend
2 spent
cr. 4 spoke
20 sport
4 stairs
10 state
cr. 1 stay
9 Steve
5 still
21 stole
17 stolen
17 Stone
20 store
1 story
15 -stories
1 *study*

21 -studied
cr. 3 Sullivan
2 *syllable
2 table
5 take
9 tax
8 tea
9 teach
8 teacher
10 team
10 teenager
4 teeth
11 test
11 tester
10 Texas
10 than
15 that's
5 there
8 these
9 third
7 thirteen
7 thirty
cr. 3 throat
19 throw
13 tie
11 time
14 timetable
12 tired
18 toast
3 today
16 told
16 Tony
20 tore
cr. 3 touch
cr. 2 train
7 tree
cr. 3 trust
13 try
12 -tried
6 TV
14 *underline
cr. 3 understand
22 union
22 United States
21 university
cr. 1 upset
22 U.S.
9 *valley*

cr. 4 violent
cr. 4 vote
22 wait
20 want
cr. 4 Washington
7 wasn't
4 water
18 way
1 we
20 wear
5 wedding
9 week
18 weekend
16 we'll
cr. 1 we're
17 what's
7 wheel
7 where
12 while
12 White
13 why
12 wife
cr. 3 wild
19 wind
19 window
15 wives
17 woke
cr. 4 won
cr. 1 wonder
17 won't
20 wore
cr. 2 worker
cr. 3 world
1 *write*
8 writer
11 written
cr. 3 wrote
10 year
18 yellow
2 yesterday
5 yet
1 York
21 young
3 your
14 you're
5 yourself
19 zero
11 zip code

© New Readers Press. All rights reserved.